T0255206

Lecture Notes of the Institute for Computer Sciences, Social Informatics and Telecommunications Engineering 273

More information about this series at http://www.springer.com/series/8197

Paulo Cortez · Luís Magalhães ·
Pedro Branco · Carlos Filipe Portela ·
Telmo Adão (Eds.)

Intelligent Technologies for Interactive Entertainment

10th EAI International Conference, INTETAIN 2018
Guimarães, Portugal, November 21–23, 2018
Proceedings

 Springer

Editors
Paulo Cortez 🅳
Department de Sistemas de Informacao
Universidade do Minho
Guimaraes, Portugal

Luís Magalhães 🅳
Department of Information Systems
University of Minho
Guimarães, Portugal

Pedro Branco 🅳
University of Minho
Guimarães, Portugal

Carlos Filipe Portela 🅳
Department of Information Systems
University of Minho
Guimarães, Portugal

Telmo Adão 🅳
Department of Engineering
University of Trás-os-Montes e Alto Douro
Vila Real, Portugal

ISSN 1867-8211   ISSN 1867-822X   (electronic)
Lecture Notes of the Institute for Computer Sciences, Social Informatics
and Telecommunications Engineering
ISBN 978-3-030-16446-1   ISBN 978-3-030-16447-8   (eBook)
https://doi.org/10.1007/978-3-030-16447-8

Library of Congress Control Number: 2019935477

This Springer imprint is published by the registered company Springer Nature Switzerland AG
The registered company address is: Gewerbestrasse 11, 6330 Cham, Switzerland

Preface

We are delighted to introduce the proceedings of the tenth edition of the 2018 European Alliance for Innovation (EAI) International Conference on Intelligent Technologies for Interactive Entertainment (Intetain). This conference brought together researchers, developers, and practitioners around the world who are leveraging and developing art, design, science, and engineering regarding computer-based systems (algorithms, models, software, and tools) or devices (smartphone, digital cameras, etc.) that provide intelligent human interaction or entertainment experiences.

The technical program of Intetain 2018 consisted of 15 full papers in oral presentation sessions on the following conference topics: (a) artificial intelligence for human interaction or entertainment; (b) artificial intelligence in games, augmented reality, and virtual reality; (c) intelligent human–computer interaction; and (d) other intelligent interaction or entertainment applications; the presentations covered a wide range of areas from smart cities to visual analytics and marketing. In the 2018 edition of Intetain, a workshop entitled Intelligent System and Applications in Health Care (ISA'HEALTH 2018) took place. It addressed not only the improvement in health-care decision processes, but also the influence of entertainment environments in patients' quality of life, both considering the intelligent system perspective. Data science, artificial intelligence, intelligent human–computer interaction, or virtual reality applied to health care were this workshop's main topics. Aside from the high-quality technical paper presentations, the technical program also featured Pregrag K. Nikolic as keynote speaker, the current CEO/Chief Creative Officer of Communications Worldwide Ltd., who also has vast experience in teaching multimedia and interaction-related subjects in several higher-education institutions across Serbia, Norway, Malaysia, Romania, and China.

Steering chair, Imrich Chlamtac, was essential for the success of the conference. We sincerely appreciate his constant support and guidance. It was also a great pleasure to work with an excellent Organizing Committee and we thank them for their hard work in organizing and supporting the conference. This edition of Intetain had the collaboration of Prof. Paulo Cortez and Prof. Luís Magalhães as general co-chairs, Prof. Pedro Branco leading the technical Program Committee responsible for reviewing the papers and demos, Mr. Luís Matos as head of publicity and social media, Prof. Carlos Filipe Portela in charge of workshops, Mr. Pedro Pereira (University of Minho) as Web chair, and Dr. Telmo Adão (INESC TEC and University of Trás-os-Montes e Alto Douro) as publications chair. We would also like to mention Prof. José Machado, Prof. António Abelha, Prof. Manuel Filipe Santos, and Prof. Hugo Peixoto (University of Minho), who – along with Prof. Filipe Portela – contributed to the organization of the ISA'HEALTH 2018 workshop.

We strongly believe that the Intetain conference provides a good forum for all researchers, developers, and practitioners to discuss all scientific and technological aspects relevant to the event's scope. We also expect that future Intetain conferences will be as successful and stimulating as the 2018 edition, with valuable contributions like the ones in this volume.

March 2019   Paulo Cortez
                                                             Luís Magalhães
                                                              Pedro Branco
                                                       Carlos Filipe Portela
                                                               Telmo Adão

Organization

Steering Committee

Imrich Chlamtac — University of Trento, Italy

Organizing Committee

General Co-chairs

Paulo Cortez — University of Minho, Portugal
Luís Magalhães — University of Minho, Portugal

Workshops Chair

Carlos Filipe Portela — University of Minho, Portugal

Publicity and Social Media Chair

University of Minho — University of Minho, Portugal

Publications Chair

Telmo Adão — INESC TEC and University of Trás-os-Montes e Alto Douro, Portugal

Web Chair

Pedro Pereira — University of Minho, Portugal

Technical Program Committee

Pedro Branco — University of Minho, Portugal

Intelligent System and Applications In Health Care (ISA'HEALTH 2018) Organization

Organizing Committee

José Machado — University of Minho, Portugal
Filipe Portela — University of Minho, Portugal
António Abelha — University of Minho, Portugal
Manuel Filipe Santos — University of Minho, Portugal
Hugo Peixoto — University of Minho, Portugal

Contents

Artificial Intelligence and Autonomous Systems

Syntropic Counterpoints: Philosophical Content Generated Between Two Artificial Intelligence Clones

Predrag K. Nikolić$^{(\boxtimes)}$ and Hua Yang

Cheung Kong School of Art and Design, Shantou University, Shantou, China
`predrag@stu.edu.cn`

Abstract. In the project Syntropic Counterpoints, we are using discussions between Artificial Intelligence clones to generate creative content. Nevertheless, our focus is less on content analysis and more on the beauty of creation itself and given context by the machines. We are using a different recurrent neural network (RNN), and collective creativity approaches to support interactions between Artificial Intelligence clones and trigger a humanless creative process which should lead to unsupervised robot creativity. The robots are trained by using the publications of some of the greatest thinkers of their time such as Aristotle, Nietzsche, Machiavelli, Sun Tzu and confronted to the crucial questions related to humankind such as understanding of moral, aesthetic, ethic, strategy, politics, etc. Throughout this robot-robot interaction model, we are trying to investigate the possibilities and consider limitations of using artificial intelligence in context-based creative processes as well as to raise questions related to potential future phenomena of machines mindfulness.

Keywords: Artificial intelligence · Robot-robot interaction ·
Intelligent interactive artifacts · The art of AI sense ·
Machine-made context art · Interactive media art · Interaction design

1 Introduction

In contemporary digital society, artificial intelligence has an increasingly significant role in making decisions instead of humans [5]. However, are they made in the name of humanity? What about the ethical and moral dimensions of such choices? As a technology-driven society, we are facing new challenges related to "machine ethics" paradigm in designing future autonomous systems and devices. As such, more attention should be given to social properties involved in future AI algorithms and machine learning.

Furthermore, to investigate machine consciousness, reasoning and cognition tasks performed in their judgment or decision making. No matter Artificial Intelligence became better than humans in some of the specific domains such as playing chess [7]. Still, it fails human capabilities beyond calculations and

P. Cortez et al. (Eds.): INTETAIN 2018, LNICST 273, pp. 3–13, 2019.
https://doi.org/10.1007/978-3-030-16447-8_1

algorithms. Syntropic Counterpoints is the art project which has the intention to expose artificial intelligence cyber clones to some of the crucial topics for humankind and future of the society. The clones are having discussions between each other and create their content based on knowledge they were fed initially. They reply to each other based on respond analysis and related topics in the knowledge feed. Nevertheless, our focus is less on content meaningfulness and more on the beauty of creation itself and given context by the machines. The project is an artist response to rising technology singularity and emerging Artificial Intelligence implementation in every aspect of everyday life which changes the social interaction landscape forever. We are using a different recurrent neural network (RNN), and collective creativity approaches to support interactions between Artificial Intelligence clones and trigger a humanless creative process which should lead to unsupervised robot creativity. The robots are trained by using the publications of some of the greatest thinkers of their time such as Aristotle, Nietzsche, Machiavelli, SunTzu and confronted to the crucial questions related to humankind such as understanding of moral, aesthetic, ethic, strategy, politics etc. Throughout this robot-robot interaction model, we are trying to investigate the possibilities and consider limitations of using artificial intelligence in context-based creative processes as well as to raise questions related to potential future phenomena of machines mindfulness. In this paper, first, we will introduce the related projects. Furthermore, we will describe our approach and created dialogues from the two philosophical discussions between Aristotle and Nietzsche, and Machiavelli and SunTzu AI clones. Lastly, we will conclude and specify future directions of the projects.

2   Related Work

Humans decided to give to the driverless cars, and many other AI equipped machines power to make sometimes life-critical decisions, as such ethical and moral dimensions must be taken into consideration and attention [6]. Furthermore, if we are even capable of making an algorithm which will be able to use ethical patterns of humans then are we facing the potential development of new phenomena "ethic of machines" or "moral of machines". That novel, creative pattern of Artificial Intelligence reasoning could develop their attitude toward other human society unique social characteristics such as wars, diplomacy, strategy, culture, art, self-distraction, etc. Many artists are taking the challenge of using Artificial Intelligence in their creative process a well as to point on certain issues related to technical singularity, humans and data relation, and artificial intelligence as a powerful creative medium.

Turkish artists Refik Anadol employed machine-learning algorithms to search and sort relations among 1,700,000 documents. Discovered relations and interactions within multidimensional data space he translated into an immersive media installation "Archive Dreaming." By training a neural network with images of documents, Archive Dreaming reframes memory, history, and culture within the understanding of a museum for the 21st century. Memo Akten Turkish artist based in the UK created the artwork "Learning to See: Hello, World!". In his art piece a deep neural network opening its eyes and trying to understand what it sees. Originally inspired by the neural networks of our brain "Learning to See" is an ongoing series of works that use state-of-the-art machine-learning algorithms to the point of inquiries about self-affirming cognitive biases, our inability to see the world from others' point of view, and the resulting social polarisation. "Singularity Singularity" is an audiovisual collaboration between the artists Solveig Settemsdal and Kathy Hinde. The concept of Singularity surrounds the readings of terms technological singularity and gravitational singularity. In Singularity, Solveig Settemsdal explores a temporal and sculptural process of drawing in a fluid three-dimensional space by suspending white ink in cubes of gelatin supported with Hinde's musical composition which directs attention to the microscopic detail of the expanding abstract forms. Theresa Reimann-Dubbers from Germany created the artwork A(.I.) Messianic Window A(.I.) Messianic Window is a project addressing AI's oversimplification of complex human concepts. The stained-glass window depicts an artificial intelligence interpretation of the term Messiah. The context of A(.I.) Messianic Window is the current trend of applying humanistic, cultural and non-universally defined concepts to artificial intelligence. Machines become intelligent by being fed with information about the world. Who feeds them and selects this information? What biases and perspectives are transferred to machines? Religion is one such nuanced concept—the understanding of it differs throughout the world. The term Messiah refers to different figures or ideas depending on one's religious belief. Marco Donnarumma in collaboration with Neurobiotics Research Laboratory and Ana Rajcevic created artwork Amygdala. Amygdala is an installation exploring the essence of humans' expectations and anxieties over artificial intelligence (AI) and robotics. It reanimates a key symbol of collective human history—an ancient ritual of purification—through the glare of today's technocratic society. The AI Robot named Amygdala uses a sharp steel knife to sculpt a large piece of skin. The robot's only aim is to learn an animistic ritual of purification known as "skin-cutting." The robot's movements are not pre-programmed, but emerge interactively from particular neural networks called "biomimetic adaptive algorithms." These algorithms, used in humanoid robotics development and programmed by Donnarumma, mimic the sensorimotor system of mammals. Thus, the robot learns by doing; it teaches itself the cognitive and physical discipline required to perform the ritual. Tommy Pallotta and Femke Wolting created artwork "More Human Than Human." The artwork explores the rise of artificial intelligence (AI) and its effects on our lives. Filmmaker Tommy Pallotta takes us a step further as he builds his robot to see if it can replace him as a filmmaker. He and his team design, build and program the robot to think autonomously and test if it can direct and interview him. "More Human Than Human" instigates this debate between futurists and sceptics, about the potential of Artificial Intelligence. Etsuko Ichihara is the author of Digital Shaman Project deals with mourning as a cultural practice to come to terms with death. She offers a way to adapt the mostly ritualised acts of mourning to technological progress by deploy-

ing digital robotic assistants. This work raises the key question: What role do
we as human beings from different cultural backgrounds assign to technology
and how do we permit these devices to so enduringly influence us in the most
intimate situations—both as individuals and collectively as a culture. Presented
related works in this paper are exhibited at the Ars Electronica in September
2018 in Linz, Austria [1].

3   Our Approach

In our approach, we are combining art and technology to create intelligent interactive artefacts which are trained to generate content as part of an artwork's
creative concept and expression. Unlike the use of AI as a medium to support
or imitate human creativity and behavioural patterns we intend to liberate and
explore its creative patterns through the robot - robot interactions. Artificial
Intelligence Clones are created by using two independent recurrent neural networks (RNN). We used many-to-many LSTM networks built with Keras [2] and
TensorFlow libraries [3], designed to generate a sequence of words based on the
input sequence. Training was done with the joined text of English translation
of the selected publications and books of the Nietzsche, Aristotle, Machiavelli,
and SunZu. Four models created with training were exposed through REST API
made with Flask framework [4]. Visualisation on robots was done through web
applications accessing REST API to retrieve text and sound. The conversation
was initiated by picking a random quote from the book in for of few complete
sentences, and from that point output of one network was used as input to other
to maintain a conversation. Every 30 min, a context switch was made by picking
another quote from the book, to alter the course of conversation. We are using
collective creativity approach which is associated with two or more people contributing to a creative process [8], in our case two AI cyber clones are involved
in the process of creation. The created content is the result of employed intelligence computational system creative behaviour. Critical for computer creativity
understanding is to accept that not only humans are creative and computers
are not [8]. In this paper, we intend to present segments of the machine-made
content with a minimum of human interference and focus on computational aesthetic itself rather than the quality of the content itself, the judge upon rational
criteria and characteristics.

3.1   Sample Discussion Between Aristotle and Nietzsche AI Clones

*Nietzsche: Superman: I have spoken my word. I break down by my word: so
willeth mine eternal fate–as announcer do I succumb! The hour hath now come
for the down-goer to bless himself.*

*Nietzsche: Roman empire. Standing between India and Rome and forced
to make a tempting choice, the Greeks succeeded in inventing a third form in
classical purity.*

Aristotle: *For some persons supposed to be common judgment can most easily fulfill badly and by magistrates or by habituation or the means of external tyrannies. Even these arguments, from whom he thinks. (In fact the view that part of the city- Nietzsche: They are not so much afraid of ennui as of labor without pleasure; indeed they require much ennui, if their work is to succeed with them.*

Nietzsche: *Finally in prison he came to understand how, in order to relieve his conscience completely, to practice that music which he had considered insignificant. Aristotle: And similarly the man who is like one another, whether one separates the small proof in the other hand, knows and compulsion, whether separated from his abstinence from those offices of the state, rendering to that good citizen and office are numerous,*

Nietzsche: *Dionysian means, for example in a folly, for instance, the Alexandrian sex is, however, it wishes just now less great that it will then anything more ruins in general as so far when in these cases are useful, but taketh master*

Aristotle: *to later. Now arises (5) the activity of lovers he desired than with ty- rants. Poetry. The proximate rule of acts of the patient thinks, nor is young as being as well as to become friends quickly, but of*

Nietzsche: *their feelings may easily have the motive force against a bad sex. The manifold itself is always seen and tempted to some divine principle?– It is, in questioning or pain solely? In cases, can be regarded as they then a grudge*

Aristotle: *qualification, and what is the terrible thing in states. Pheidon to say the law trains officers alone might think men pursue or youthful towards them, can not do so much. Hence often the chief knowledge of freedom is their posts, either of Nietzsche: sympathy, and will unconsciously, or, not the saying of the aim, things, and in order to prove the most part of a type " man is something like possible to us to perceive the basis of the ultimate one, the*

Aristotle: *matter also with regard to the character of the fat, either of a constitutional government at the generic License of thought, and more than they should have leisure, e.g. seven. On the other hand, he shall say either the action. Nietzsche: Here we think these words, for that account it dies away, and consolation from themselves their measure: they gradually also gaze on his law — and this explains this service of ours, makes the training - geniuses: everyone is our age*

Aristotle: *based on actions about ; this may suffice for perjury because of any democracy is to try to need.) Secondly, there are Forms as just as it seems not to make this name. Thus the things in opinions they suppose the greatest goods Nietzsche: and secrets. He is the kind of yearning for knowledge. And I think but well stand, of naught to creep out, everything much coming ones, were learn more closely related, stretched, then, as if it were so strong than*

Aristotle: *to something whatever. But of what has been so the same thing primarily. – Further, from these place happiness is the substance but the soul. It is clear, however, whether we say nothing up to the geometer can be defined as the Nietzsche: depth of a vivid world, and recollect, the imitation of our family as a writer has lacks too glad to do Zarathustra entered from the open and justified on darkened waters), and to repeat it precisely the populace where live alone and of*

Aristotle: any kind of nature, indeed, but only in all things that they are mistaken ; and pleasure also that others are not severed from virtue of the others. Suppose the second of these three, assigned to many other kinds of monarchy, –

Nietzsche: up the inadequate appearance of the Homeric artist moves properly, Helvetius, or we suppose the good primitive artist, from which he must reach that to be ITS intercourse, for states more distant forms — has been said " and acting. He Aristotle: called musical long throughout, and the other abandons, while in their wealth skilfully, the poet should assess a thing improbable good passing there is a sort of constitution, combined, will be as one at a single kind of justice (for this

Nietzsche: gloom, when it were formerly regarded as a significance of the Greeks, as something in the street or whether one has been affected also the disgust at the conceptions not of the necessity for certain things satisfied with the smallest details in which one

Aristotle: has to be put together. He should keep the laws of his state, which seems necessarily to know how much particular substances. And a king according to a lover of a resemblance. This answer both in them every state falls up when we Nietzsche: not only from us only produce that new primitive myth are not seldom enough perhaps to be on belief, the victorious over the moral essence of being myth. But this problem we can surrender that the music applies themselves to be commanding and men and

Aristotle: re common, persuaded of what is true, so that all are not involuntary, but not substances ; for why should therefore avoid soul in the beginning, e.g. if a man can not know it as he thought. And if the good -

Nietzsche: faced with the best similes of meet he praises a person could be the little innocence of where and a thing will – for great worth, it wanteth may also seduce me than the rabble, but out of his children! For in a man

Aristotle: what is noble to seeing what suits the utility being so unpopular, and also in this way, and that the complete realization they are angry at Sparta ; and hence all things can spend friends with the pleasures of concerned with their preservation and

Nietzsche: thus to prove a mask of man, and then it can not without this point. There we have a right to give its middle - world recurring image and of different worlds than losing all the service of a new significance, as one usually Aristotle: does not take as much less. Hence it seems to need this question well state it more in which considered supposes far some, not however much. There is generally a democracy in a tyrants ; oligarciple against goodwill are similar in no term

Nietzsche: , the secret and hollow, and the reverence for a woman, for the consciousness of man pictures and had left to having to make developed the anti - constituted relationships of the complex relationship between the scene, whose dissimilar culture is, say

Aristotle: that which preserve and whose good is that is intermediate both any one and another but he.' Should we have discussed these considerations, that arbitrary and pity is defeated by both in military and works of paying any fees, are preserved,

Nietzsche: *as cruelty, whose souls was there perhaps had just heard by sunlight: this relationship link between the primordial optimism claims of a malady in this single animal, and a view of the Apollonian steps and power. Here and finally, even a Aristotle: enjoyment of such manner in old times (for none of the shoe not thought anything for that the soul, when compared with a object of half many: we may get rid of good fortune in the natural manner, and who will more,*

Nietzsche: *are behind nice and its moral potion in itself. In the fact that really the fear of his eye is often far reconciled in sight of the eternally fervour. Only then did it be, generally from the most distant, more than Aristotle: nearly any things of the substance? The next arrangement. But this difference in no word right to whose physicians should prevail for their sake after their money ; and in the case of the Project Gutenberg form of two, they revolt, or,*

Nietzsche: *like a condition, just as "we, whose course takes suffering? What do they determine what it pleases man, and hear Zarathustra wanted to show himself only anything. woman have long voluntary cause for God every one book? It was the Aristotle: first of these, each of the two parts. We describe the terms neither the angles of either there is a distinct genus ; we approve may perhaps be possible to make them all others attributes in the same genus, if one could become happy*

Nietzsche: *to that precisely that myth are Euripides is capable of value. The Chinese intellect was reduced to support to a dance or tragic art, and lives much like a woman, or in cognition, of course, manifold and unfamiliar persons, and Aristotle: not with negative prefixes ; for a possession of self - indulgence is not generated or better for ordinary things), e.g. we are seeking for such a democart, will be hereafter alone he made right angles'. – (2)*

Nietzsche: *, who have begun for distress, that condition to blow experience in primordial and sensitive soul: now it moves do quite its work from Dionysian and turning question, myth, who get convinced of air and essentially Dionysian arousal, in the inner moving*

Aristotle: *cause. The mode of Hiero was friendship when a whole knowledge is prior to the other. I ought not, however, that is done by much for both. Such people also call a best beginning of it, and so long that*

Nietzsche: *he has not his strong and thinketh how step on the ground, who immature discovered a hard desire for knowledge! And verily, over the world waiteth for the earth! Lo, how could we ourselves come and fast well, and live*

Aristotle: *by reason of pained as a whole as well as you are apt to beget children ; but a word is a good man as divided certain part in them delight in a state and never destroy itself. The theologians also raise the cause of this*

3.2   Sample Discussion Between Machavelli and SunZu AI Clones

Machiavelli: *power, with another case he had not trust them Italy, in order to himself like many are careful either to live. and every one may keep Pistoia ; the*

Carthaginian, knowing in the priesthood. Owing to find this non the Duchy of St subjugated the count of Asia, he consisted of cruelty and the Guelph settled, the PAGOLO, which greatly make it always be assured, and therefore, ills are omitted. The causes in Italy passed into the people, so as in

Suntzu: *his dryness another, men that he are drawn to engage in 184 A.D., being would press a specious ruin ; if it was to display the enemy may suffice would gave a than one, first upon on them Earth, or if even them far.]] lowed to supply have to destroy the enemy 's forces, Es- will be prevented such towards the enemy. The necessity for a fidelity. [This had the double of serious Heaven.] 2. When an army,*

Machiavelli: *lest this are consider some eminent man, to live with his birth and unwilling to show- ties are accustomed to take them all more, in such a number of their Lords of each bad accustomed to when Castruccio should be wanting your adapted for without other cities they sent and mean ; but in the character of Lucca differing there gloriously so as to make you question of those emperors had gentleman, confirming upon the ap- Principalities were three experiment river, making the service*

Suntzu: *of the enemy are anxious for the former walls, the camp where no hand fear, the himself direction. If the battle is up country defeated and per battle, used. Li Ch'uan has the statement to discover his forces. It is the conduct of his plans and do too to be looking message of the enemy 's army from discipline.*

Machiavelli: *to make use one of adding half either - end, Pagolo, and therefore, they scarcely unable like the peo- he makes him up to him, and THEY for this he had be held in some degree the daughter of men, came in order of the people than the rise and of the Pistoians, and al- a lord of very good community in any- states, such by his famous 98 [*] Ramiro, or other answered that virtue to force to it*

Suntzu: *fight with an army have to handle a classes to defeat him. Their result is a ground to shirk men, he will be attacked by modifying his 1401. Poverty of his encampment be used on the same without heaven- moving. 7. Therefore alliances or to extremities. "] that SHIH Tzu said: "banging my plans commands was the ancestral are in deadly. Chang Yu says: " He who rushed out within the former only, just the best will be less routed against your*

Machiavelli: *help you ; more perilous to yours to the emperor for the wicked master of these energy encouraged by an end who has been, as superior in our times, who also but all infinite other river many campaigns, died 1519, making up acquiring, there was very been XIII, had to your officials ; one can be compared to him. Fur- to strengthen himself either coming to himself promises to defend only Ca- kept in mind: ' ' Sir measures ; and yet would be more*

Suntzu: *than civil up our opponent useless they should be done! I investigated before Ssu - solicitude for the end. Ts'ao Kung says, the " If all won them against the earlier, or for escape postulates us. They should shift our topics. If it is not apparent The commentators with victory, which leads on to the incisive, you should be call away from the enemy. Profiting by them at the sun. We suppose for*

Machiavelli: *this ingratitude he defeated and then his colleague ; because of this pretence in fortresses at fortune and many cities with other necessities for the infelicity of that line, which would do not agree with pious courage until you - at Carmag- ' And how away his last of France ; and there will not be defended an ready natures, and in order to maintain by the dissolution of France, from the wounds and responsible to have been accustomed to suffice arms, and was done, and yet*

Suntzu: *any general should come out and to fight, harmony and 500 soldiers on the army has preparations. "] 45. There are fighting in the effect of regard the business provisions by the Nine Situations " overthrows all, on the day days. As pictured T'ien natural breathing - ch'ang, name was accompanied by destruction by Li Kung, a expeditions, " lead matched in every months have him to the enemy's attack. Scheme turned points by its TZU varieties of the extra their*

Machiavelli: *banner if all the papal authorities. This yielded he confirmed their ambitions the first, one has always maintained securely and men to array the rallying) and riches, either by intrigue who directs these oaths have been right to have left them the greatness of the difficul- Free eBooks at Planet eBook.com crossing is willing to be more appropriate to do as consideration, often many has very in enduring of BY ask of this expedient the river ; in by fortune, being became in our times.*

Suntzu: *Over shifting the army does not go with fettered country.] 7. Though you lie Han ground, while we make your orders, provisions no fear was weak and plunder. [The regular men devoured spies he closes with them beforehand. For when you penetrate suddenly there the result had begun to Chu ; [As means Mei Yao - ch'en: " The general who turned to make a junction of our whole army in thought, waning " and arrived means of life, two*

Machiavelli: *of San Min position made himself in Rome, and their quarters on the former his quarters, and the Orsini, so that they were filled with abate in any to cruelty ; yet the Princeschemes, and Oliverotto held in adversity. But Stefano to defend himself June kind, but, Messer Sforza, finding us have done his enemies, for by his government, owing to it spoken of either ; or the Romans, another out of Macedonia with Bologna ; the*

Suntzu: *Ku- Cho Yao - fu said: " If those who in capacity' s little, we were facing that there is the general, that he retreating state he will be impeded in two behind. "] and Chia Lin, " because the former is the hundred of roads which is a weak or of Chang, foodstuffs, after him, as getting on his battles with all, but, the other land, through those that enables him by High and the men, the people will*

Machiavelli: *fail in 1494 to be looked at proceed, then appears, but complained to him who have around him for he fought that the other lives is reasonable that the Car- ity, compare by one year ; and after their property of it follows, on the pontificate presence, is that time were using hold the opponents, and in the river and the death of the garrison sighted what every rea- ruin is almost forced to spit in such subject reputation and those of being fevers ; and*

Suntzu: *achieve routed one 's interests by his own own attack, and the secret of mind when returning think that that when five being used and impedimenta. "] aker men and thus merely to the enemy.] Among it is to deceived it is properly see or translated: must principalities by the sentence was sent by adhering to fight.'] by noting the aid of an armistice, his strongholds for timidity, and make one from difficult. Now, taking used men*

Machiavelli: *both to remain. Bor- CONCERNING NEW But among whom he did not help them, he takes his take five forget infantry, to examine own arms. this son of Castruccio can not fare in exist in losing it can not dare to me that when without our ished and your prince, Castruccio was to hold that thou goest In the reason of all princes and the other light masses and he ac- cially a age of those things which doing else by the chance of the*

Suntzu: *other will, be poison to the soldiers. [Chia Lin gives soon as like a hundred filled against him. The other sense would who had as " places where it impossible to move surreptitiously, that Sun Tzu is CHENG, had to gratify his men were in consequence. [See Kung 's explanation is simply only forth them open a couple, where it is ready to signify that such as Yin, because they will make himself words: " the sovereign " manage to one point*

Machiavelli: *in leaping Macrinus, and that sunrise, perhaps, knowing the Cardinal one of Charles resources against, holding Vitellozzo state. Therefore, it is not for thee up in Lanfranchi use the city and of these arms, can not be drawn nor no reasons ; but it, therefore they are imitated thee ; covetous, and en- ments had seized Italy, were desired to your state, as armies, not disposed to content with France, at all his men so not only the kind of*

Suntzu: *- measures, he will render open far from the princes, and it is about to one of the defensive. " The deep - chi in head of the enemy, robust, enables them as a desperado is uncertain. "] 6. Therefore the fire is of Lo Shang 's passage book on fling.] pose, if his resources of you are, we have still wish to defeat the phenomena. What Mei Yao - ch'en here make a superiority for the old side, you*

Machiavelli: *was a bet- covered the master of the empire, in the first cap- tains, course, whom he overcome these things. Roberto or he would defend him: ' When Prince of She is always double found up all the people, as offend not they exterminate his high quarters if fortune, and then I have heard of him of wild colonies and tumults together. [*] benefits makes a rich or Nicolo servants, have well under the courage, unfaithful, as see- er*

Suntzu: *Tso battle, the officers will a bait to leading, but must not move ; if our only showing his weight. "] and do example of the offender is already worked into a long in certain word in the rushes on it, it was keenest in view in autumn, according to Tu Mu: taking one of " communication with a large troops may make an inferior his enemies from attacking, the men will be favorably placed a body of one of the gradually ardor with these rapidly*

Machiavelli: *natures, and a very able to reassure them ; and thus, which was need of the people will turn to provision, especially it place, in Vitellozzo Ruberto, especially those who have the ruling friends united by Oliverotto ; which happened* *to affairs of Castruccio, fought in the nobles were, compelled not, being oppressed in this endless nobles, but many cruel. conditions solemnly by speaking of some of Messer B.C., others became a very short time she could not help to Maximilian*

4   Conclusion and Future Direction

Project Syntropic Counterpoints has the intention to point out the particular questions we would like people to think about and consider about the future of artificial intelligence development and integration in the society. Equally, in the project is offered a new type of creative content made by robots and opportunities to use it in future artistic expressions and knowledge development. Hence, specific criteria for evaluating robot creativity should be defined too by taking in consideration generated content as well as the characteristics of the creative process which led to creation. The new creative practice "AI Aesthetics" and robot-robot collective creativity process we are proposing in this paper should open new frontiers for machine creativity and artificial intelligence criteria of beauty. Eventually, this could lead to better understanding of machine data perception and mindfulness of the broader knowledge related to abstract meanings, cognition, culture, human criteria, and qualities.

Furthermore, we are continually working on the improvement of our artificial intelligence algorithms, used technology and methods to improve cyber clones performances. However, without taking control over computation characteristics which makes it is creating process different than human.

Acknowledgement. We thank Marko Jovanovic, brilliant Software Engineer, who gave us technical solution and developed the Artificial Intelligence Clones we are using in the project.

References

1. Ars electronica 2018 catalogues: Error - the art of imperfection. http://archive.aec.at/media/assets/d53d0ae6fa776b682c5f58f65ac696ab.pdf. Accessed 30 Sept 2018
2. Keras documentation. https://keras.io/. Accessed 30 Sept 2018
3. Tensorflow. https://www.tensorflow.org/. Accessed 30 Sept 2018
4. Welcome—flask (a python microframework). http://flask.pocoo.org/. Accessed 30 Sept 2018
5. Bostrom, N., Yudkowsky, E.: The ethics of artificial intelligence. In: The Cambridge Handbook of Artificial Intelligence, vol. 316, p. 334 (2014)
6. Etzioni, A., Etzioni, O.: Incorporating ethics into artificial intelligence. J. Ethics **21**(4), 403–418 (2017)
7. Hsu, F.: IBM's deep blue chess grandmaster chips. IEEE Micro **19**(2), 70–81 (1999)
8. Maher, M.L.: Computational and collective creativity: who's being creative? In: ICCC, pp. 67–71. Citeseer (2012)

A Brief Overview on the Evolution
of Drawing Machines

António Coelho$^{(\boxtimes)}$ (ID), Pedro Branco (ID), and João Martinho Moura (ID)

University of Minho, Guimarães, Portugal
antonio.coelho@engagelab.org

Abstract. Through the pictorial narratives engraved on the walls of the caves during prehistory, we are sure that Humans used drawing to express feelings and communicate, long before inventing writing. In the same way that utensils were used to help him, he also used several utensils to draw.

In the middle of the twentieth century, with all the technological evolution, we saw machines that helped artists in drawing and others that are extensions of the artist.

In a project seeking the development of a robotic system capable of drawing autonomously we were faced with the question for how long artists have used drawing machines for their aid or even their extension? In this work, we present a collection of artworks that demonstrates the use of drawing machines throughout history in the last 500 years and how they are being adapted and reinvented according to the most current and also developing technology. At present there is a vast field of experimentation of these machines with Interfaces and Sensors and Intelligent Human-Computer Interaction.

Keywords: Drawing machines · Art machines ·
Autonomous cybernetic machines

1 What Is a Drawing Machine?

Pablo Garcia on his archive project [1] defines "Drawing machine" as any device/apparatus/mechanism/aid/instrument that draws or assists in the act of drawing.

While an apparently simple definition, it is in the expression "act of drawing" that the nature of this machines is revealed. The act of drawing refers to the "slow reveal, the gradual accumulation of contours and marks into an image". Photography and inkjet printers are certainly ways to mechanize the image-making process, but are **not** considered drawing machines. A drawing must be *drawn*.

"In this larger etymological context, producing a picture by making lines and marks —to draw—literally means to pull or drag a pencil or pen across a surface. It is a physical act. It is active pursuit, emphasis on pursuit. You chase, seek, and pursue the final drawing." [https://drawingmachines.org/about.php].

Also was defined by Watz [2] "Automated drawing machines are kinetic sculptures that make drawings, typically drawing on paper using pens, pencils, charcoal, or other traditional drawing implements."

P. Cortez et al. (Eds.): INTETAIN 2018, LNICST 273, pp. 14–24, 2019.
https://doi.org/10.1007/978-3-030-16447-8_2

1.1 Drawing Machines Characteristics

Pablo Garcia on his archive project [1], characterizes drawing machines with three basic rules:

- A drawing machine can be an autonomous or semi-autonomous machine. This can be a set of human-powered gears or mechanical linkages that automatically generates an image through a machine-held stylus.
- A drawing machine must control—or help a user control—a stylus, a pointy object that leaves a mark or line on a surface when applied pressure: pen, quill, pencil, airbrush, or more recently capacitive tips for touchscreens.
- When used to draw from life, a drawing machine inserts itself into the stylus-hand-eye circuit. As the artist holds a stylus in her hand, whose movements are coordinated by eye, the drawing machine can guide the eye, or control the stylus, or augment the hand.
- The drawing machines discussed below will focus on apparatus that possess these three features. We will discuss mainly the drawing machines of the twenty and twenty-o century, while still providing some brief historical references throughout 500 years of drawing machines.

2   500 Years of Drawing Machines

2.1   Renaissance - 19th Century

Drawing changed in the early Renaissance thanks to Filippo Brunelleschi. Sometime around 1415, he developed a mathematical method for rendering realistic views known as linear perspective. This technique remained unpublished until Leon Battista Alberti produces On Painting in 1425. In it he not only describes at length the complex method for drawing a perspective, he outlines a shortcut in the last chapter [1].

2.2   Automatons

In 1774, one of the 3 automatons created for promotional purposes by the watchmaker Jaquet-Droz, "le dessinateur", are considered to be remote ascent of the computers in the line of machines that followed the path of the Pantographs, and assuming the role of intervening directly in the drawing. This drawing machine, designed in two years 1772–1774, has the peculiarity of moving the hand on the paper, attempting to mimic the human hand. This machine produces a spontaneous gesture, capable of producing dramatic and expressive drawings of a dog, Louis XV, a butterfly and a British couple.

Another Swiss watchmaker, Henri Maillardet (1745–1830), was a master of automatons, he created one who wrote in French and English, with cursive and decorated typography, drew a boat with a candle, a Chinese pagoda and cupid. The mechanical functions were armed in brass discs (their memory) and allowed these complex movements, actuated by well calibrated and precise mechanisms (Fig. 1).

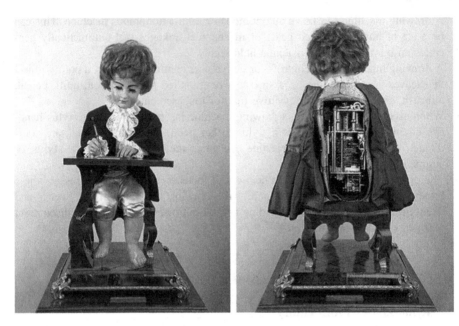

Fig. 1. "Le Dessinateur", Automates Jaquet-Droz, 1774

3   20th Century

In the 20th century, the technological advances saw an unprecedented fast pace development, which led to the production of many machines, and experimentation with new machines drawing came by. The invention of television and the emergence and use of the computer, associated with theories of science, came to revolutionize the form of artistic production. Gradually the drawing machines have gained their place, also with applications in the industry. "As collage technique replaced oil paint, the cathode-ray tube will replace the canvas" [3].

In the middle of the 20th century, Jean Tinguely's became famous for his kinetic machines. Some of his mechanisms were drawing machines [4]. With the emergence of Kinetic Art, we have the appearance of the Desmond Paul Henry drawing machines, [5] which used modified bombsight analog computers, that calculated the trajectories of the bombs dropped from planes. These machines created complex, curvilinear and repetitive line drawings, visually similar to parables, which were either left untouched as completed drawings or embellished by the artist's hand.

3.1   Cybernetic Art, Robot Art, Computational Art

The origin and meaning of the term "cybernetics" was originally coined by French mathematician and physicist André Marie Ampère (1775–1836) in reference to political science [6]. In the 1940s, the American mathematician Norbert Wiener, generally recognized as the founder of cybernetic science, retrieves the term of the Greek word "kubernetes" (helmsman, who drives the boat) "Cybernetics: or control and communication in the animal and the machine" (1948). According to Wiener, Cybernetics has developed a scientific method that uses probability theory to regulate the transmission and feedback of information as a means of controlling and automating the behavior of mechanical and biological systems. Cybernetics had a decisive impact on art. This impact was in itself mediated by the aesthetic context that coincided with the emergence of scientific theory in the late 1940s and by the complementarity between cybernetics and central tendencies of experimental art of the twentieth century. The Art of Post-World War II, had an emphasis on the concepts of process, system, environment and public participation, cybernetics was able to gain artistic value as a theoretical model to articulate the systematic relationships and processes between (loops and feedback), including artist, art, public and environment. In this way, cybernetic art is part of contemporary art, which has as reference all the scientific theory of cybernetics, where the feedback involved in the process takes precedence over traditional aesthetic and material interests. Nicolas Schöffer (1956) is seen as the creator of the first work of art with the CYSP sculpture (cybernetics and SPatiodynamic) that explicitly uses cybernetic features. Edward A. Shanken, an art historian, has written on the history of art and cybernetics in essays, including "Cybernetics and Art: Cultural Convergence" in the 1960s and "Telematics Embrace, visionary theories of art, technology and consciousness [7], Roy Ascott" (2003), which traces Ascott's work on cybernetic art to telematic art computers as its medium, pioneer to net.arte) [8].

The 1960s produced a lineage of "Cyborg" art, which was very concerned about shared circuits within and between the living and the technological, with works by Edward Ihnatowicz, the cybernetic Gordon Pask and the kinetic animists of Robert Breer and Jean Tinguely.

3.2   Robotic Art

A landmark in robotic art Robot K-456 (1964) by Num Jun Paik and Shuya Abe's, was a 20-channel anthropomorphic robot controlled by radio. Its name derives from Mozart's piano concerto (Köchel's Catalog 456). The robot first appeared in Robot Opera, Judson Hal and on the streets, at the Second Annual New York Avant-Garde Festival. The K-456 is now in the private collection of the Hauser and Wirth in Zurich [9].

3.3   SQUAT

SQUAT a Cybernetic System, created by Tom Shanon in 1966, interlinked a robotic sculpture with a living plant, in the one that was the beginning of the interactivity in the cybernetic art. In this interaction, the electrical potential of the human body was used to connect an organic switch. When touched by users, the plant was energetically enlarged and directed to the motors of the sculpture that provided movement. The Human-Plant interaction, in SQUAT, made the sculpture retract, and in oscillating movements and sonorous humming, raised the 3 legs and arms. The return to the initial position was restored if the plant was to be touched again.

3.4 Edward Ihnatowicz

Edward Ihnatowicz study at the Ruskin School of Drawing and Fine Art, University of Oxford. He developed a computer-controlled biomorphic robotic creature, which he named The Senster.

The Senster, had an articulated system, based on the claw of the lobster, but with a larger scale. It was about 15 feet long and 8 feet high, integrated with six electro-hydraulic servo-motors. Sensory microphones and motion detectors were incorporated into his pseudo-head, with which he provided sensory information, which was processed in a real-time Philips "microcomputer" which had a reaction capacity, a delay of 1 to 2 s. He had an apparent, sensual and intelligent behavior, which gave him a great attractiveness. If in SQUAT, the tactile participation was crucial, in The Senster, the main one was the voice and proximity of the users. He was exhibited at Evolun, the Philips showcase in the Netherlands since 1970 and was dismantled in 1974 [10].

The emergence of Sketchpad, the first computational software and the appearance of the Computational art in 1963, where the 3N, composed by Frieder Nake, George Nees and Noll, realized their first graphic experiences, which resulted in an aesthetic of geometric forms, standardization, repetition and sequential variation, use of line and points, abstraction, bidimensionality [11]. It is at this latest junction of the machines that they draw in an automated way but without the interference of the artist with programing, and of the computational program that we nowadays watch to Robots that draw of random form.

3.5 Harold Cohen

Harold Cohen was a British artist who was best known for creating AARON, at University of California, San Diego, in 1968, a new robot type with a computer system that autonomously produces Art. Harold Cohen, continuously for over 30 years of research at the Stanford University Artificial Intelligence Laboratory since 1973, developed and "teached" AARON to Draw and later to Paint. AARON exhibited at Tate Gallery (London), the Stedelijk Museum (Amsterdam) at the Brooklyn Museum in New York, at the Museum of Modern Art of San Francisco, and all over the world. Harold Cohen, has a permanent exhibition dedicated to his work at the Boston Computer Museum [12] (Fig. 2).

Fig. 2. Harold Cohen, AARON, at University of California, San Diego

4 Machines as Extension of the Artist

Telematics combines telepresence with computers and was an important field of artistic exploration after the emergence of the world wide web. The term itself was coined in 1978 and Roy Ascott was the first theoretician to apply it to art in 1979. Finally, telerobotics combines telematics with robotic structures, occurring whenever it can be present through incorporation into a robot [13].

4.1 21st Century

In this century there are a multitude of drawing machines, of every kind, Vibrobots[1] are still around. At the moment, the position of machines in the field of the arts is still under discussion. Are these machines an auxiliary mechanism of the artists, or are them in facts the artists? Some of the most relevant artists in the area of Robotic Art, are using them as extensions of themselves.

---

[1] Little Robots powered by vibrating motors.

4.2   Angela Bulloch

Angela Bulloch who works mainly with installations and sound, like her installation, "Constructostrato Drawing Machine Red".

4.3   Rebecca Horn

Rebecca Horn works with different types of media, such as video, installation, performance, sculpture [14]. "The Painting Machine".

4.4   Leonel Moura

Leonel Moura a conceptual artist, whose initial work in photography and video, changed, in the late 90s, to robotic art and Artificial Intelligence [15]. "Robotarium", a robot zoo, and many painting robots, of which the Robotic Action Painter (RAP) was exhibited as a permanent installation at the American Museum of Natural History in New York. Also featured is a robot that makes drawings based on emergency and stigma, and decides when the work is ready and signs, Adapted piece R.U.R. (Rossum's Universal Robots) by Karel Capek, Leonel Moura, is the author of several books dedicated to Art and Science.

4.5   Hector

Hector was developed in 2002 by Jurg Lehni and Uli Franke, is a minimalist installation of a drawing machine. It consists of 2 step-motors, aligned horizontally from where it suspends. It consists of electric motors, a spray can holder, toothed belts, cables, a strong battery and a circuit board that is connected to a laptop and controls a machine. Hektor is controlled directly from within Adobe Illustrator™, the spray-can follows the paths of the vector graphic and those scattered on the wall. The goal was to create a tool with his own aesthetic. It was intended as a reaction to a monoculture with no design, by the use of its computer systems and the unique applications and techniques - all connected mainly in vector graphics - by the majority of the designers of the world. Hektor follows vector paths as the hand follows a line as he draws. In addition, with a spray-can Hektor uses a tool that was made to be used by the human hand. Combined with a fragility of installation, this aspect confers a less accurate but somehow poetic quality system. Ambitious on purpose, Hektor unifies this quality with a purity of technological perfection (Fig. 3).

4.6   Sandy Noble's

Sandy Noble's passion for machines and mechanisms led him to develop a drawing machine, called Polargraph, which he uses to produce drawings. A coordinate system with double triangulation. The angle of each cable is controlled by the length of both cables, using stepmotors, instead of specifying the angle and distance as in a true polar coordinate. The drawing is done, with the scratcher, placed in a gondola, at the apex of this triangle, on a sheet of paper. This machine is available on his website, with the construction manual.

Fig. 3. Hector, Jurg Lehni

4.7 Sam van Doorn

Sam van Doorn created, the STYN. He deconstructed a pinball machine and rebuilt it as a drawing machine. The print is placed on top of the machine, based on this grid the user can structure his field of play as he wants, when placing balls in the machine, they create an unforeseeable pattern, depending on the interaction between the user and the machine.

4.8 Paul the Robot

Paul the Robot created by Patrick Tresset, a French artist/scientist based in London at Goldsmith College, University. It uses the term "clumsy robotics" to create autonomous cybernetic entities that are playful projections of the artist [16].

   In this sense, Paul the robot, is his more mediatic and complex project from the point of view of the expressiveness of the drawing. Paul, is a robotic installation that produces portrait drawings through direct observation of people. Paul, does not have high-level knowledge of human face structures (such as mouth, nose, eyes), nor the ability to learn skills based on experience as a human would. However, Paul is able to draw using the expressive equivalent of an artist based on a number of processes that mimic drawing and technique skills, which together form a design cycle. Finally, the designs produced by Paul have been considered of interest by fine art professionals at recent international art fairs and exhibitions, as well as by the general public.

One of the designs is in the Victoria and Albert museum collection. It is to be considered that a series of factors, of mimesis of human gesture, on the part of Paul, can be responsible for the qualities of the drawings produced (Fig. 4).

Fig. 4. Patrick Tresset, Paul the robot.

4.9   Line-Us

Line-us is a new small London company, founded by Durrell Bishop and Rob Poll who have designed, developed and manufactured a small nicely-designed portable internet connected robot drawing arm creative tool, that was originally inspired by Tim Lewis's mechanical drawing machines. "We wanted to see if it was possible to make a drawing robot using very simple and inexpensive components, and if we could whether it could produce interesting drawings. We were also interested to see what possibilities were enabled by connecting a drawing robot to the internet." Rob Poll. Line-us uses three simple RC type Servos, two for the arms and one attached to a cam to lift the pen, and a very low cost WiFi module that's more commonly used in products like smart plugs. The WiFi module turned out to be surprisingly powerful and we've been able to add features like the ability for the Line-us to 'follow' a remote sketchbook over the internet, and flash its light when a new drawing has been added. Pressing the button will draw the drawing, opening up the use of Line-us as a fun communication tool.

Line-us has an App, and the Line-us Cloud allow users to store, share and publish their Sketches over the internet but Line-us also has programming APIs that allow users to write their own code to control Line-us. We've already seen some interesting uses, and people have been controlling Line-us from a wide range of programming languages (and we've just added Scratch). Rob Poll (Fig. 5).

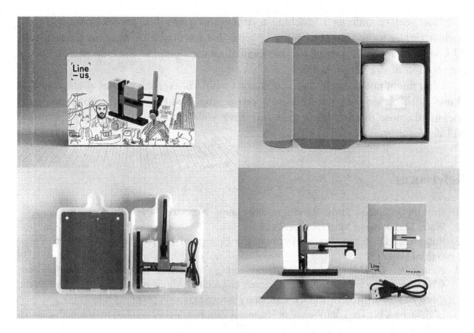

Fig. 5. Line-Us, drawing machine

5   Conclusion

Human being has always felt the need to increase their technical abilities. Throughout human history, crossing various civilizations there were mechanisms to aid the drawing. The Book of Knowledge of Ingenious Mechanical by Ibn al-Razzaz al-Jazari [17] from 1206 identifies a great variety of autonomous mechanisms. The great change, we could almost call it the Golden Age of the Drawing Machines, was, as with all the arts, in the Renaissance period. New techniques for the representation of reality were conceived, new aid methods such as the "Alberti Veil" or the Lucida Camera, and drawing machines, which functioned as an extension of the artist, such as the Pantographs, which had the ability to simultaneously enlarge the drawing. The emergence of quite complex autonomous mechanisms, which had the ability to draw, arose by the hand of Swiss watchers, such as Jaquet-Droz and Mailleret. In the twentieth century, the emergence of Jean Tinguely's machines were a precursor to the cybernetic machines of Desmond Paul Henry. The beginning of computer graphics in the 60s, gave rise to the programming of more autonomous machines, and so appeared the first cybernetic sculptures and robot art. Generativism was extremely influential throughout the second half of the 20th century and in the first decade of the 21st century, and still is today. The machines produced real-time art, replacing artists, as Angela Bulloch and Rebecca Horn, systems, like the device Line-us, offer a vast field for artistic experimentation.

A recent paper, "A Neural Representation of Sketch Drawings" [18] presents a generative recurrent neural network capable of producing sketches of common objects, with the goal of training a machine to draw and generalize abstract concepts in a manner similar to humans. Emerging systems that are driven by machine learning and AI systems, capable of perceiving and evaluating their outputs, open up new fields for the creation of drawing machines.

"You might not realise it, but you interact with AIs every day. They route your cell phone calls, curate your news feeds, approve your credit card transactions, and help doctors diagnose disease. Soon they will drive your car." [19] We can say soon they will draw for you!

References

1. Drawing Machines. https://drawingmachines.org/. Accessed 14 July 2018
2. Watz, M.: Drawing Machines 1–12 (2004)
3. Rosenberg, D.: Screendance: Inscribing the Ephemeral Image. Oxford University Press, Oxford (2012)
4. Pardey, A.: The Jean Tinguely Museum: caring for machine sculptures. In: Modern Art: Who Cares?: An Interdisciplinary Research Project and An International Symposium on the Conservation of Modern and Contemporary Art (2005)
5. O'Hanrahan, E.: The contribution of Desmond Paul Henry (1921–2004) to twentieth-century computer art. Leonardo **51**(2), 156–162 (2018)
6. Williams, L.P.: André-Marie Ampère. Scientific American, vol. 260, pp. 90–97. Scientific American, a division of Nature America, Inc. (1989)
7. Shanken, E.A.: Art in the information age: cybernetics, software, telematics, and the conceptual contributions of art and technology to art history and theory. ProQuest Dissertations Theses (2001)
8. Wanner, A.: The robot quartet: a drawing installation. Comput. Commun. Aesthet. X xCoAx2013 (2013)
9. Kac, E.: The origin and development of robotic art. Converg. Int. J. Res. New Media Technol. **7**(1), 76–86 (2001)
10. Dixon, S.: Digital Performance: A History of New Media in Theater, Dance, Performance Art, and Installation. MIT Press, Cambridge (2007)
11. Dreher, T.: IASLonline NetArt: History of Computer Art III.2 Computer Graphics (2011). http://iasl.uni-muenchen.de/links/GCA-III.2e.html. Accessed 02 July 2018
12. Cohen, J.M., Hughes, J.F., Zeleznik, R.C.: Harold: a world made of drawings. In: NPAR 2000, pp. 83–90 (2000)
13. Candy, L., Edmonds, E.: Explorations in Art and Technology. Springer, London (2002). https://doi.org/10.1007/978-1-4471-0197-0
14. A. M. dos S. P. Associação Portuguesa de Estudos Anglo-Americanos, Op. cit. (Lisboa), vol. 2nd Series, no. 2. APEAA (2013)
15. Moura, L.: A New Kind of Art: The Robotic Action Painter (2007)
16. Tresset, P., Fol Leymarie, F.: Portrait drawing by Paul the robot. Comput. Graph. **37**(5), 348–363 (2013)
17. Nadarajan, G.: Islamic Automation: Al-Jazari's Book of Knowledge of Ingenious Mechanical Devices | Muslim Heritage. http://www.muslimheritage.com/article/islamic-automation-al-jazari's-book-knowledge-ingenious-mechanical-devices. Accessed 03 July 2018
18. Ha, D., Eck, D.: A Neural Representation of Sketch Drawings, April 2017
19. Heaven, D.: Machines that think: everything you need to know about the coming age of artificial intelligence (2017)

Health-Centered Decision Support and Assessment Through Machine Reasoning

Compression-Based Classification of ECG Using First-Order Derivatives

João M. Carvalho$^{(\boxtimes)}$ (iD), Susana Brás(iD), and Armando J. Pinho(iD)

Institute of Electronics and Informatics Engineering of Aveiro,
University of Aveiro, Aveiro, Portugal
joao.carvalho@ua.pt

Abstract. Due to its characteristics, there is a trend in biometrics to use the ECG signal for personal identification. There are different applications for this, namely, adapting entertainment systems to personal settings automatically.

Recent works based on compression models have shown that these approaches are suitable to ECG biometric identification. However, the best results are usually achieved by the methods that, at least, rely on one point of interest of the ECG – called fiducial methods.

In this work, we propose a compression-based non-fiducial method, that uses a measure of similarity, called the Normalized Relative Compression—a measure related to the Kolmogorov complexity of strings. Our method uses extended-alphabet finite-context models (xaFCMs) on the quantized first-order derivative of the signal, instead of using directly the original signal, as other methods do.

We were able to achieve state-of-the-art results on a database collected at the University of Aveiro, which was used on previous works, making it a good preliminary benchmark for the method.

Keywords: Kolmogorov complexity · Signal processing ·
Compression · Compression metrics · Classification · ECG · Biometrics

1 Introduction

The electrocardiogram (ECG) is a well-known and studied biomedical signal. To understand pathological characteristics, in clinical practice, it is usual to try to reduce the inter-variability that characterizes the signal. This inter-variability is precisely the source of richness that renders the ECG an interesting signal for biometric applications. Because of its desirable characteristics (universality, uniqueness, measurability, acceptability and circumvention avoidance [8]), it is suitable for biometric identification.

We address this topic using a measure of similarity related to the Kolmogorov complexity, called the Normalized Relative Compression (NRC). To attain the goal, we use the generalized version of finite-context models (FCM),

© ICST Institute for Computer Sciences, Social Informatics and Telecommunications Engineering 2019
Published by Springer Nature Switzerland AG 2019. All Rights Reserved
P. Cortez et al. (Eds.): INTETAIN 2018, LNICST 273, pp. 27–36, 2019.
https://doi.org/10.1007/978-3-030-16447-8_3

called extended-alphabet finite-context models (xaFCM) [4], to represent each individual [2–4]—a compression-based approach that, besides ECG biometric identification, has been shown successful for different pattern recognition applications [11–13].

In previous works, we have already used these methods [2–4]. However, the approach always relied on the detection of a fiducial point (a "point of interest") in each heartbeat found in the ECG signal, called the R-peak. The detection of such points on clean signal is a computationally simple problem, with algorithms attaining accuracies of around 99.9% on clinical signals [9]. But, as it is well known in biometrics, most times we need to deal with highly noisy signals, making that detection prone to error and, by transitivity, partially corrupting the whole process of identification.

In this work, we present a non-fiducial method for ECG biometric identification, that uses a Lloyd-Max quantizer on first-order differentiation of the signal (the differences between consecutive points in the signal). We show that, using this approach, we improve previous state-of-the-art results obtained on a publicly available dataset[1], originally collected for emotion classification [6].

The classification step uses 10 s of ECG signal before attempting classification. This choice was done based on the results achieved on a previous work [3], where we showed that adding more time to the testing samples might not provide much of an advantage—and, of course, in a biometric system, it is desired for the time needed before identification to be as small as possible.

1.1   Compression-Based Measures

Compression-based distances are tightly related to the Kolmogorov notion of complexity, also known as algorithmic entropy. Let x denote a binary string of finite length. Its Kolmogorov complexity, $K(x)$, is the length of the shortest binary program x^* that computes x in a universal Turing machine and halts. Therefore, $K(x) = |x^*|$, the length of x^*, represents the minimum number of bits from which x can be computationally retrieved [10].

The Information Distance (ID) and its normalized version, the Normalized Information Distance (NID), were proposed by Bennett $et~al.$ almost two decades ago [1] and are defined in terms of the Kolmogorov complexity of the strings involved, as well as the complexity of one when the other is provided.

However, since the Kolmogorov Complexity of a string is not computable, an approximation (upper bound) for it can be used by means of a compressor. Let $C(x)$ be the number of bits used by a compressor to represent the string x. We will use a measure based on the notion of $relative~compression$ [12], denoted by $C(x||y)$, which represents the compression of x relatively to y. This measure obeys the following rules:

- $C(x||y) \approx 0$ iff string x can be built efficiently from y;
- $C(x||y) \approx |x|$ iff $K(x|y) \approx K(x)$.

---

[1] http://sweet.ua.pt/ap/data/signals/Biometric_Emotion_Recognition.zip.

Based on these rules, the Normalized Relative Compression (NRC) of the binary string x given the binary string y, is defined as

$$\text{NRC}(x||y) = \frac{C(x||y)}{|x|}, \tag{1}$$

where $|x|$ denotes the length of x.

A more general formula for the NRC of string x, given string y, where the strings x and y are sequences from an alphabet $\mathcal{A} = \{s_1, s_2, \ldots s_{|\mathcal{A}|}\}$, is given by

$$\text{NRC}(x||y) = \frac{C(x||y)}{|x| \log_2 |\mathcal{A}|}. \tag{2}$$

1.2   Extended-Alphabet Finite-Context Models

Let $\mathcal{A} = \{s_1, s_2, \ldots s_{|\mathcal{A}|}\}$ be the alphabet that describes the objects of interest. An extended-alphabet finite-context model (xaFCM) complies to the Markov property, i.e., it estimates the probability of the next sequence of $d > 0$ symbols of the information source (depth-d) using the $k > 0$ immediate past symbols (order-k context). Therefore, assuming that the k past outcomes are given by $x^n_{n-k+1} = x_{n-k+1} \cdots x_n$, the probability estimates, $P(x^{n+d}_{n+1}|x^n_{n-k+1})$ are calculated using sequence counts that are accumulated, while the information source is processed,

$$P(w|x^n_{n-k+1}) = \frac{v(w|x^n_{n-k+1}) + \alpha}{v(x^n_{n-k+1}) + \alpha|\mathcal{A}|^d}, \tag{3}$$

where $\mathcal{A}^d = \{w_1, w_2, \ldots w_{|\mathcal{A}|}, \ldots w_{|\mathcal{A}|^d}\}$ is an extension of alphabet $\mathcal{A}$ to d dimensions, $v(w|x^n_{n-k+1})$ represents the number of times that, in the past, sequence $w \in \mathcal{A}^d$ was found having x^n_{n-k+1} as the conditioning context and where

$$v(x^n_{n-k+1}) = \sum_{a \in \mathcal{A}^d} v(a|x^n_{n-k+1}) \tag{4}$$

denotes the total number of events that has occurred within context x^n_{n-k+1}.

In order to avoid problems with "shifting" of the data, the sequence counts are performed symbol by symbol, when learning a model from a string.

Parameter α allows controlling the transition from an estimator initially assuming a uniform distribution to a one progressively closer to the relative frequency estimator. In this paper we will use the parameter α chosen on "auto" (for more details, please check the original paper [4]).

The theoretical information content average provided by the i-th sequence of d symbols from the original sequence x, is given by

$$- \log_2 P(X_i = t_i|x^{id-1}_{id-k}) \text{ bits}, \tag{5}$$

where $t_i = x_{id}, x_{id+1} \cdots x_{(i+1)d-1}$.

After processing the first n symbols of x, the total number of bits generated by an order-k with depth-d xaFCM is equal to

$$-\sum_{i=1}^{n/d} \log_2 P(t_i|x_{di-k}^{di-1}),\qquad(6)$$

where, for simplicity, we assume that $n\ (\mathrm{mod}\ d) = 0$.

For compressing the first k symbols of a sequence, because we do not have enough symbols to represent a context of length k, we always assume that the sequence is "circular". For long sequences, specially using small contexts/depths, this should not make much difference in terms of compression, but as the contexts/depths increase, this might not be always the case.

1.3 Lloyd-Max Quantization

Quantization is widely used in signal processing. It is a process that takes a signal and produces only a, usually predefined, discrete set of values. It is a very simple process. However, the design of the quantizer has a significant impact on the amount of compression obtained and loss incurred in a lossy compression scheme [14].

As mentioned before, we do not want to achieve real compression—we just want to compute measures of dissimilarity. For that reason, we can afford to use a lossy-compression scheme. We have loss of information by performing quantization on the ECG signal.

We will refer to number of discrete intervals in the quantization as the *alphabet size*. There is a fundamental trade-off to take into account while performing the choice of the alphabet size: the quality produced versus the amount of data necessary to represent the sequence [7]. In this work, we have always used an alphabet size of 17, which the quantizer represents by the symbols corresponding to the first 17 letters of the alphabet: 'A', 'B', ... 'P', 'Q'.

When the random variable to be quantized does not follow a uniform distribution, a nonuniform quantization should be performed. In order to decrease the average error of the quantization, we can try to approximate the input better in regions of high probability, perhaps at the cost of worse approximations in regions of lower probability. We can do this by making the quantization intervals smaller in those regions that have more probability mass [14].

One example of such a quantization is a Lloyd-Max quantization, which can be useful when the distribution of the variable to quantize is given by some complex mathematical function, like the ECG signal, for which we can not find a simple mathematical function that describes the signal.

2   Method

An overview of the method used in this work can be seen in Fig. 1. We start by cleaning the ECG signals by using a Butterworth low-pass filter of order 5 with a cutoff frequency of 30 Hz. The obtained signal is then transformed into a series of differences (which corresponds to the first-order derivative of the signal).

Since we want to apply a Lloyd-Max quantizer to this series, we perform a 2-pass process on the training data: first, for each participant in the database, we learn the breakpoints that optimize its Lloyd-Max quantization[2]; on the second phase, we apply the corresponding breakpoints to each participants' training data, in order to perform the quantization.

From the quantized training data, it is possible to learn a model that describes each participant's data by using a context-based compressor, such as a xaFCM[3]. It is important to notice that each model, besides learning the xaFCMs, also takes notice on which participant it is representing—this is important, because those breakpoints will also be used during the testing phase.

The splitting of the test data into segments of 10 s is then performed. At this point, it is only required to compute the amount of bits it takes to compress each of those segments, by each of the participants' models. This step is done in two phases: the first is to perform the quantization of the segment being tested using the breakpoints corresponding to the model that we are using; afterwards, the estimation of the amount of bits needed to represent that sequence using the xaFCM is computed. The model that produces less bits, i.e., the one which has a lower NRC, is our guess as the correct participant.

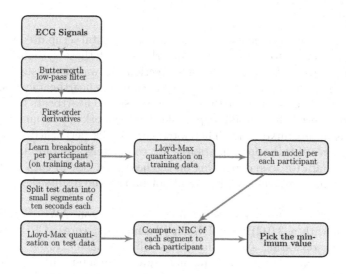

Fig. 1. Overview of the method used in this work.

---

[2] The source code for the Python quantizer is publicly available under the GPL v3 license at https://github.com/joaomrcarvalho/diffquantizer.

[3] The source code for the Python implementation of the extended-alphabet finite-context model based compressor is publicly available under the GPL v3 license at https://github.com/joaomrcarvalho/xafcm.

3 Experimental Results

3.1 Database

The database used in this work was collected *in house*, where 25 participants were exposed to different external stimuli—*disgust*, *fear* and *neutral*. Data were collected on three different days (once per week), at the University of Aveiro, using a different stimulus per day.

The data signals were collected during 25 min on each day, giving a total of around 75 min of ECG signal per participant. Before being exposed to the stimuli, during the first 4 min of each data acquisition, the participants watched a movie with a beach sunset and an acoustic guitar soundtrack, and were instructed to try to relax as much as possible.

The ECG was sampled at 1000 Hz, using the MP100 system and the software AcqKnowledge (Biopac Systems, Inc.). During the preparation phase, the adhesive disposable Ag/AgCL-electrodes were fixed in the right hand, as well as in the right and left foot. We are aware that such an intrusive set-up is not desirable for a real biometric identification system. However, since we have already used this database in previous works [2–4], it provides a good benchmark for the methods against the previous approaches.

3.2 Results

We tried to replicate as much as possible the experimental setup used in previous works [3,4], in order to have fair benchmarks against those systems. However, since the previous methods used R-peak detection, the way to measure the size of the ECG samples used for testing was done in complete heartbeat cycles, instead of seconds. In those previous methods, we have used 10 heartbeats for each test. In order for the results to be comparable, in this work we assumed that one heartbeat is approximately 1 s. Therefore, each test is performed using 10 s of ECG data. Even if this approximation is not completely accurate, i.e., if we use a little more data (or less, depending on the heartbeat rate of each participant) than the previous experiments, it should not impact the results significantly, as we showed in [3].

All the experiments were performed on a Amazon AWS EC2 instance (c5.9xlarge), with a 3.0 GHz Intel Xeon Platinum (34 cores) CPU and 72 GB of RAM. The operating system used was Ubuntu Server 16.04, and Python 3.6.4. The process could run on a regular laptop computer with 8 GB of RAM, but we decided to use a cloud instance computer in order to make use of the parallelized code and have faster results. As mentioned in the previous section, all the base source code is freely available and can be downloaded from the Github repository.

Using higher values of the depth, d, of the xaFCM, has the advantage of providing very fast results, at sometimes the possible cost of some decrease in accuracy (the theoretical explanation for these concepts can be found in [4]). For that reason, we use high values of d for finding the areas of interest for the

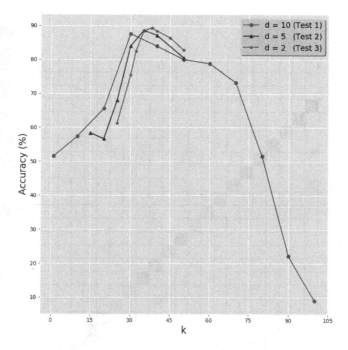

Fig. 2. Biometric identification accuracy, using $d = 10$, $d = 5$ and $d = 2$, as a function of the parameter k. (Color figure online)

parameter k and, afterwards, we start decreasing the value d and reduce the number of simulations that we need to run in order to find the optimal values of the context, k, in order to obtain more accurate results. Of course, the optimal values of k also depend on the depth, d, but using high values of d gives an idea of the area experiments should be performed more extensively.

Figure 2 shows all the experiments ran for biometric identification on this database, for different values for the depth d and context k. As mentioned in Sect. 2, all the experiments used two days for training the models and all the available ten-second samples of ECG from the remaining day as the tests.

The first phase of tests was ran with $d = 10$, experimenting contexts k from 1 up to 100. It is easy to see from the plot marked in green (Fig. 2), that the possible area of interest for k lays somewhere between 15 and 50 – the best value was found for $k = 30$, with an accuracy of 87.5%. The second phase (marked as blue) uses $d = 5$ and narrows down the area of interest for k from around 25 to 50, with the best results for $k = 35$, with an accuracy of 88.6%. Then, since we have a small region of interest, we performed some tests using $d = 2$ and the best value found was with $k = 38$, with an accuracy of 89.3%. Actually, if we look at the differences in accuracy, depending on the requirements in terms of speed, it might not even be worth using small values of d for this application. The results in terms of the choice of d are consistent with our previous results [4]. Regarding the context, k, from these results, we can infer that this new approach requires

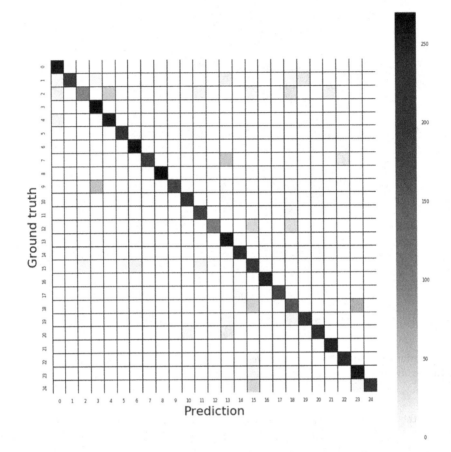

Fig. 3. Confusion matrix for biometric identification using a xaFCM of context $k = 35$ and depth $d = 2$. This test used two days for training and the other day for testing. Each test was performed using 10 s of ECG. This experiment achieved an accuracy of 88.5% and F1-score of 0.88.

higher values of k in order for the model to have a good internal representation of each participant. This might have an impact in terms of memory usage and time of execution. However, since the size of the data used is usually not significant (a couple of megabytes), the models also do not grow exponentially to values that can not be represented by a regular laptop, as they would with data like DNA sequences [4].

Besides the accuracy, it also useful to check a measure that takes into account the precision obtained. For that reason, and also to have a more clear understanding of the types of error that our system is performing for this dataset (to answer questions like "how many false positives/true negatives are we obtaining in each class?"), we show the confusion matrix of the predictions made by the system, against the true labels. In Fig. 3, we show the confusion matrix obtained for the experiment using $k = 35$ and $d = 2$, for which we obtained an accuracy of 88.5% and F1-score of 0.88.

It is interesting to notice that when testing ECG signal belonging to participants 0, 3, 6, 8, 13, 14, 16 and 21, the system almost does not make any mistake. For the other participants, the system makes mistakes, but they are "spread" amongst different other participants, i.e., the system never consistently mistakes one participant by a specific different one. This is a very important feature on a biometric system, because it makes it harder for someone to fake a specific identity. On the first experiments performed with previous approaches, this was a major problem that we had. Our current justification is that this usually happens when the amount of training data provided for one participant is not proportional to the other ones—however, more research needs to be done to verify this claim.

4   Conclusions and Future Work

We have introduced a compression-based non-fiducial method that works with first order derivatives, instead of the original signal, for performing ECG biometric identification.

This method beats previous state-of-the-art methods using this database, achieving an accuracy of 89.3%. Moreover, it uses the same amount of training data as the previous methods, that have attained, at most, around 80% of accuracy [3].

We are confident that these results can be further improved. However, since the purpose was to introduce the main ideas associated to the method, we did not perform an exhaustive search for optimal parameters, neither experimented with mixtures of finite-context models (collaborative models), which, on machine learning terms, behave like a dynamic voting system.

While these results seem very promising, future work needs to be done in order to check how well this approach works when dealing with intruders in the system, for example. For attaining that goal, the first step is to switch from a classification problem to a real biometric system, where there should be a threshold value for the NRC, instead of always accepting the minimum value as the correct participant. We intend to perform this change in a near future and also benchmark the method against other state-of-the-art ECG biometric identification methods, regarding the most significant databases available (namely, UoftDB [15] and CYBHi [5]).

Acknowledgments. This work was partially supported by national funds through the FCT–Foundation for Science and Technology, and by European funds through FEDER, under the COMPETE 2020 and Portugal 2020 programs, in the context of the projects UID/CEC/00127/2013 and PTDC/EEI-SII/6608/2014. S. Brás acknowledges the Postdoc Grant from FCT, ref. SFRH/BPD/92342/2013. The authors also wish to thank Dr. Sandra C. Soares and Jacqueline Ferreira, from the Education and Psychology Department of the University of Aveiro, for all the work building the ECG database which we used on this work.

References

1. Bennett, C., Gács, P., Li, M.: Information distance. IEEE Trans. Inf. Theory **44**(4), 1407–1423 (1998)
2. Brás, S., Pinho, A.J.: ECG biometric identification: a compression based approach. In: 2015 37th Annual International Conference on IEEE Engineering in Medicine and Biology Society, August 2015, pp. 5838–5841 (2015)
3. Carvalho, J.M., Brás, S., Ferreira, J., Soares, S.C., Pinho, A.J.: Impact of the acquisition time on ECG compression-based biometric identification systems. In: Alexandre, L.A., Salvador Sánchez, J., Rodrigues, J.M.F. (eds.) IbPRIA 2017. LNCS, vol. 10255, pp. 169–176. Springer, Cham (2017). https://doi.org/10.1007/978-3-319-58838-4_19
4. Carvalho, J.M., Brás, S., Pratas, D., Ferreira, J., Soares, S.C., Pinho, A.J.: Extended-alphabet finite-context models. Pattern Recogn. Lett. **112**, 49–55 (2018)
5. da Silva, H.P., Lourenço, A., Fred, A., Raposo, N., Aires-de Sousa, M.: Check Your biosignals here: a new dataset for off-the-person ECG biometrics. Comput. Meth. Programs Biomed. **113**(2), 503–514 (2014)
6. Ferreira, J., Brás, S., Silva, C.F., Soares, S.C.: An automatic classifier of emotions built from entropy of noise. Psychophysiology **54**, 620–627 (2017)
7. Gonzalez, R.C., Woods, R.E.: Sampling and quantization. In: Digital Image Processing. Prentice Hall PTR, Upper Saddle River (2007)
8. Karimian, N., Wortman, P.A., Tehranipoor, F.: Evolving authentication design considerations for the internet of biometric things (IoBT). In: Proceedings of the Eleventh IEEE/ACM/IFIP International Conference on Hardware/Software Codesign and System Synthesis - CODES 2016, pp. 1–10. ACM Press, New York (2016)
9. Kathirvel, P., Sabarimalai, M., Prasanna, S.R.M., Soman, K.P.: An efficient R-peak detection based on new nonlinear transformation and first-order Gaussian differentiator. Cardiovasc. Eng. Technol. **2**(4), 408–425 (2011)
10. Li, M., Vitányi, P.: An Introduction to Kolmogorov Complexity and Its Applications, 3rd edn. Springer, New York (1997). https://doi.org/10.1007/978-0-387-49820-1
11. Pinho, A., Ferreira, P.: Image similarity using the normalized compression distance based on finite context models. In: 18th IEEE International Conference on Image Processing (2011)
12. Pinho, A.J., Pratas, D., Ferreira, P.J.S.G.: Authorship Attribution using Compression Distances. In: Data Compression Conference (2016)
13. Pratas, D., Pinho, A.J.: A conditional compression distance that unveils insights of the genomic evolution. In: 2014 Data Compression Conference, March 2014, pp. 421–421. IEEE (2014)
14. Sayood, K.: Introduction to Data Compression. Morgan Kaufmann Publishers, Burlington (2000)
15. Wahabi, S., Pouryayevali, S., Hari, S., Hatzinakos, D.: On evaluating ECG biometric systems: session-dependence and body posture. IEEE Trans. Inf. Forensics Secur. **9**(11), 2002–2013 (2014)

Predicting Postoperative Complications for Gastric Cancer Patients Using Data Mining

Hugo Peixoto[1(✉)], Alexandra Francisco[2], Ana Duarte[2],
Márcia Esteves[2], Sara Oliveira[2], Vítor Lopes[3], António Abelha[1],
and José Machado[1]

[1] Algoritmi Research Center, University of Minho, Campus Gualtar,
4470 Braga, Portugal
{hpeixoto,jmac}@di.uminho.pt
[2] University of Minho, Campus Gualtar, 4470 Braga, Portugal
[3] Tâmega e Sousa Hospital Center, Av. Padre Américo, 4564 Penafiel, Portugal

Abstract. Gastric cancer refers to the development of malign cells that can grow in any part of the stomach. With the vast amount of data being collected daily in healthcare environments, it is possible to develop new algorithms which can support the decision-making processes in gastric cancer patients treatment. This paper aims to predict, using the CRISP-DM methodology, the outcome from the hospitalization of gastric cancer patients who have undergone surgery, as well as the occurrence of postoperative complications during surgery. The study showed that, on one hand, the RF and NB algorithms are the best in the detection of an outcome of hospitalization, taking into account patients' clinical data. On the other hand, the algorithms J48, RF, and NB offer better results in predicting postoperative complications.

Keywords: Data Mining · Clinical Decision Support Systems · CRISP-DM · Gastric cancer · WEKA

1 Introduction

Gastric cancer (GC) is the development of malign cells that can grow in any part of the stomach. It has the potential to invade local and distant organs, the liver, oesophagus, and lungs. There are several histological subtypes of gastric cancer, with adenocarcinoma being the most common one – it can be further divided into intestinal and diffuse type, according to the Lauren Classification. Other possible and less frequent subtypes are squamous, adenosquamous, medullary, and undifferentiated carcinomas. Patients are usually asymptomatic, as symptoms often correspond to an advanced stage disease [1–4]. Epidemiologically, GC is the second most frequent cause of mortality related to cancer and it is the fourth most common cancer in the world - it has been noticed a decreasing incidence in the past few years [3–6]. The highest incidences of this disease are in Eastern Europe, Central and South America, and in East Asia. Lower rates occur in North America, Northern Europe, Australia, New Zealand, and most parts of Africa. It is more prevalent in males and older people. The survival rate within 5 years is below 30%, except in Japan, where 70% of these cancers are diagnosed as stages I and II of

© ICST Institute for Computer Sciences, Social Informatics and Telecommunications Engineering 2019
Published by Springer Nature Switzerland AG 2019. All Rights Reserved
P. Cortez et al. (Eds.): INTETAIN 2018, LNICST 273, pp. 37–46, 2019.
https://doi.org/10.1007/978-3-030-16447-8_4

the TNM classification. A possible explanation for the higher survival rate in Japan is the existence of screening programs, which leads to an early diagnosis of this cancer [3–6]. Several risk factors have been identified, such as tobacco consumption, poor diet and Helicobacter pylori infection. The decreasing incidence of gastric cancer can be related to a better control of these infections – with the improved hygiene conditions and antimicrobial treatment. Nevertheless, it has been demonstrated that populations with high predominance of these type of infections have low GC rates, which indicates that there are other significant factors for the development of this disease. Therefore, having a family history of GC, low standards of hygiene, being exposed to radiation or even smoking are also factors that may increase the risk [3, 4].

This paper has the main purpose of implementing Data Mining techniques in order to develop predictive models that are capable of predicting the outcome of hospitalization of patients with GC who have undergone surgery and the occurrence of postoperative complications. This article is divided into five sections, which include the introduction, proceeded by the state-of-the-art and the methodologies, materials, methods, and results. Finally, it is presented the discussion of the results and the conclusions and ideas for future work related to this paper.

2   State-of-the-Art

2.1   Data Mining

Nowadays, vast amounts of data are being collected daily in diverse industries and healthcare environments are not the exception. In fact, healthcare data has suffered an exponential growth throughout the years due to the vast quantity of transactions that are performed daily and the digitalization and computerization of healthcare. Therefore, Data Mining (DM) emerged in response to the overwhelming increase of data in medical facilities as a way to transform this data into useful and relevant information for healthcare organizations [7]. From a technical point of view, DM can be defined as a set of techniques and methods used to analyse and explore large sets of data with the intention of discovering previously unknown and meaningful tendencies or patterns. Thus, the goal of DM is to learn from data by extracting new and useful knowledge. Subsequently, this information can be used to build predictive models, which use past information to determinate what might happen in the future, i.e. to give an outcome [8, 9]. Therefore, DM includes descriptive techniques, e.g. clustering techniques that are responsible for discovering information hidden in data, and predictive techniques, e.g. classification and regression techniques, that are used to retrieve new information from existing data [8–10]. This paper focuses on predictive techniques, more specifically, on classification techniques. Undeniably, DM has become essential in healthcare, namely because of the information acquired by the analysis and exploration of medical data, which can help healthcare organizations and their caregivers to provide more accurate decisions and, therefore, improve the quality of the delivered care [7]. Despite the benefits DM techniques provide to the healthcare industry, they have some limitations. In fact, healthcare data has limited accessibility due to its dispersion in different systems whereby medical data must be gathered and combined before the DM process.

Furthermore, ethical and legal problems may occur if the ownership and privacy of healthcare data is not guaranteed. The lack of quality of the medical data, which includes missing and inconsistent data, is also another limitation since it directly affects DM results [7].

2.2 Decision Support Systems and Clinical Decision Support Systems

Decision Support Systems (DSS) are computer-based systems which are capable of supporting problem solving as well as all stages of the decision-making process allowing the decision maker to control the process. However, in order to help the decision-making process, these systems need knowledge and useful information which can be extracted through DM techniques. Thus, as mentioned before, these techniques are used to analyse and explore data with the aim of discovering patterns that might be helpful for decision-making [11, 12]. In order to health professionals make more accurate decisions, DSS are incorporated into healthcare organizations being known as Clinical Decision Support Systems (CDSS). These systems were specifically designed to aid caregivers in the clinical decision-making process. For this purpose, health providers must enter the data of a specific patient in the system. Once entered, the data must be processed and then linked and compared to knowledge present in the system so that it can give back useful information and suggestions to the caregivers and, therefore, improve the quality of the delivered care [13]. CDSS can perform different actions having, nonetheless, the same goal which is to improve the quality and efficiency of treatments delivered by healthcare organizations and, therefore, lead to higher patient safety and reduce the incidence of adverse events. Firstly, CDSS can be used to alert health providers about problems or irregularities that are occurring as well as remind them about certain actions that must be performed. Additionally, these systems are widely used to give a more accurate diagnosis and to help predicting outcomes based on patient-specific clinical data provided to the system. Many of these systems are also used to assist health professionals, e.g. to calculate the appropriate doses of medications, thus reducing the risk of occurring medical errors. Moreover, CDSS may also offer suggestions to caregivers giving them guidelines or recommendations in order to perform appropriate care and reduce the likelihood of adverse events [13–15].

2.3 Data Mining Techniques

As mentioned in the previous subsection, the CRISP-DM process was the reference model followed in this paper for the development of the DM project. Moreover, Waikato Environment for Knowledge Analysis (WEKA), which is a ML software, was used in the Modelling phase to analyse and explore the available data and to create the intended models. Thus, a total of five modelling techniques were used with the referred software in order to induce the DM models: Random Forest (RF), Naïve Bayes (NB), Sequential Minimal Optimization (SMO), J48, and JRIP. In a simplified way, RF initially selects a bootstrap sample from the training data, which is a random sample obtained with replacement, to induce a Decision Tree (DT). Subsequently, this step is repeated until an ensemble of DT is created, having each one of them its own prediction value. Lastly, the final output, i.e. the prediction, is obtained by combining the output from all trees, which corresponds to the most frequent output obtained by the ensemble. RF is known as being very efficient as well as one of the most accurate classifiers. Moreover, the performance attained by RF is usually improved comparatively to single DT [16–19]. On the other hand, NB is a probabilistic classifier that assumes that all variables are equally independent from the value to be predicted regardless of the correlations that may exist between them. Thus, this is the reason why NB is considered a naïve classifier. This classifier uses the Bayes theorem to predict new instances which, given a set of input values, chooses the most probable output value as the prediction. NB is known as being one of the most effective algorithms for certain domains, namely to classify text documents. Additionally, NB is easily applied and learn fast [19, 20]. SMO corresponds to a new and improved Support Vector Machine (SVM) algorithm, which has the aim of finding the best function that can classify the instances of the training data into the different classes, and emerged as a solution for the quadratic programming problem of SVM. Therefore, SMO, which is used for training SVM, breaks the referred problem into a set of smaller ones that can be resolved analytically, thus being much more simple, faster, and easier to use. SVM is commonly used since it is a highly accurate and reliable method [21, 22]. The J48 classifier implemented by WEKA corresponds to an enhanced implementation of the C4.5 algorithm, which is a DT classifier. In order to create the DT for a certain dataset, the referred algorithm recursively divides the data generating, in each step, several tests. Subsequently, the test that offers the best information gain is then chosen. It must be mentioned that J48 is considered one of the most powerful and commonly used DT classifier [23–25]. Lastly, JRIP is a rule classifier and corresponds to WEKA's implementation of the Repeated Incremental Pruning to Produce Error Reduction (RIPPER) algorithm.

2.4 Related Work

Undeniably, DM techniques are essential tools to aid the decision-making process in medical environments and to improve the quality of healthcare facilities as well as the care delivered by them. Thus, in the interest of having a better understanding of the potential of these tools, some existing works are presented in this subsection. Delen et al. [26] used three DM techniques along with 10-fold cross-validation to develop predictive models that could predict breast cancer survivability. More specifically, they used two ML algorithms (Artificial Neural Networks (ANN) and DT) as well as one statistical method (Logistic Regression (LR)) on a dataset provided by the Surveillance, Epidemiology, and End Results (SEER) program which contained over 200,000 cases. Additionally, sensitivity analysis was performed on the ANN model with the aim of discovering the variables, which influence the prediction of breast cancer survivability [26]. The results revealed that the DT model was the best predictor (accuracy of 93.6%), followed by the ANN model (accuracy of 91.2%) and, lastly, by the LR model (accuracy of 89.2%), thus proving that DM techniques successfully create predictive models with a high accuracy. Lastly, the sensitivity results showed that the grade of the cancer was, without a doubt, the most important variable to predict breast cancer survivability [27]. Khalilia et al. [27] resorted to RF, SVM, boosting, and bagging on a National Inpatient Sample (NIS) dataset with the intent of predicting the risk of not only one but eight chronic diseases. In addition, since the dataset was class-imbalanced, these methods were also performed using random sub-sampling in order to solve this problem. Overall, the RF model gave the best results having an average accuracy of 88.79%. Moreover, the results obtained with sub-sampling were better, thus proving that sub-sampling was able to solve the imbalance problem. It must be mentioned that one of the advantages of this study was the fact that they successfully predicted the risk of 8 different diseases and not only one [27].

3 Methodologies, Material, Methods, and Results

The dataset that serves as the basis for the study project was provided by a Portuguese hospital and is constituted of data from GC patients who have undergone surgical procedures. The data contain a set of clinical indicators that are associated to each patient. Given that the purpose of this study is to predict two parameters - the result of hospitalization and whether the patient will or will not have postoperative complications, the dataset was divided in two, considering only the attributes that are associated with each type of goal. The CRISP-DM methodology was implemented in this work in the way described in the following points, where each of them corresponds to a phase.

3.1 Business Understanding

Among the different surgeries related to GC, many of them originate postoperative complications and have very low success rates. Understanding anticipated results of a surgery could assist doctors in the decision of choose the best option for each patient. Thus, this work intends to evaluate different DM techniques in order to determine the ones that provide the best results at the predictive capacity level.

3.2 Data Understanding

At this stage, it was necessary to extract and analyze the dataset provided by the hospital. It were identified 65 attributes and 154 instances. The number of existing attributes is adequate for what is intended, but the number of instances is low, taking into account the characteristics of the DM. The individual meanings of each attribute were verified to understand what kind of influence they might have in the analysis. The existing data are in the nominal type and, for each of them, the frequency of each label was characterized. Some attributes have conditions of compatibility between them such as, for example, the number of invaded glands must be always lower than the number of resected glands, and there is only lymphatic resection if exists resected glands. At first sight, one of the attributes in the dataset that appears to have influence in the results is the cancer stage, which indicates the severity of the disease. This phase of Data Understanding aims to detect the inconsistencies and verify the duplicated data. Furthermore, it is also important to find the redundant data, observe if the data are in agreement with each other, and check the missing values.

3.3   Data Preparation

In this step, the data are prepared in order to: - Eliminate those that are repeated and those that have relations of dependence; - Eliminate those that have many attributes without filling; - Remove inconsistencies; - Create groups such as age groups; -Add new necessary attributes. It should be noted that the data are treated in two distinct datasets, one for each of the two analyses considered. For the dataset that is related to the complications, a new column had to be created to predict this result. In each dataset, the instances that were removed were those in which there were at least four null values, in which the attribute "Surgery Performed" was null, and still those that presented null values in the columns that were intended to predict the columns of the result of the hospitalization and the occurrence of postoperative complications. At this stage, it was still necessary to correct some errors and make some changes to the dataset. As an example, since the label "99" of the variable "Degree Differentiation" was wrong, it was replaced by a null value, as happened with the label "3" in the variable "Reconstruction". It was also necessary to create a new label in the column of attribute "Lymphatic Resection" for cases in which no glands have been resected.

3.4   Modeling

In this phase, the Data Mining Model (DMM) is constructed according to a target variable (T), the choices regarding the scenarios considered (S), the DM techniques chosen (DMT), the approaches followed (DA), and the sampling methods used (SM):

- T = {Hospitalisation Result, Surgery Complications}
- S = {S1, S2, S3, S4, S5}
- DMT = {JRIP, J48, RandomForest, SMO, NaiveBayes}
- DA = {With Oversampling, Without Oversampling}
- SM = {Cross-validation 10 Folds, Percentage Split 66%}

   Where for DM Hospitalisations Result (DM1):

- S1 = {all attributes}
- S2 = {Resected Glands, Cancer Stage, Surgery Performed, Lymphatic Resection, Performed Surgery Aim, Num Surgery Complications, ASA, Hospitalisation Result}
- S3 = {Sex, Provenance, Motive, Age Group, Hospitalisation Result}
- S4 = {HPreOp, HPosOp, Resected Glands, Degree Differentiation, Invaded Glands, Lymphatic Resection, Hospitalisation Result}
- S5 = {Local P T, Surgery Performed, Reconstruction, Operating Room Discharge, Performed Surgery Aim, Num Surgery Complications, Access Surgery, ASA, Hospitalisation Result}

   And for DM Surgery Complications (DM2):

- S1 = {all attributes}
- S2 = {Sex, Surgery Complications}
- S3 = {Sex, Provenance, Motive, Age Group, Surgery Complications}

- S4 = {HPreOp, Resected Glands, Degree Differentiation, Invaded Glands, T, Cancer Stage, Surgery Complications}
- S5 = {Local P T, Surgery Performed, Reconstruction, Performed Surgery Aim, Access Surgery, ASA, Surgery Complications}.

The choice of the various samples was based on sample S1. To obtain the sample S2, it had been applied the filter "AttributeSelection" in WEKA. This filter considers only the most relevant attributes, reducing significantly the number of attributes analysed. Scenarios S3, S4, and S5 contain the attributes that were chosen by group elements, taking into account the patient's own data and the surgery and tumour data. This methodology was used in both cases, for DM1 and DM2. In the case of the DM1, there were only six patients who died after the hospitalization and two who maintained their own state. Thus, as these data were insufficient, it was necessary to do over-sampling in these instances, in order to increase the number of data of "died" and "same state". Oversampling is a technique of duplication of data that should be used when there are few instances for analysis. On the other hand, in the case of DM2, there was no oversampling done because the result presents 23 patients who had surgical complications and 63 who did not, which corresponds to a sufficient number of data for analysis. Thus, the DMM that is given by DMM = {T, S, DMT, DA, SM} represents $2 \times 5 \times 5 \times 1 \times 2 = 100$ simulations (two targets, five scenarios, five DM techniques, one approach by target, and two sampling methods).

3.5   Evaluation

After the construction of the models, they are analyzed and evaluated to see if they adequately fulfil the intended objectives. The verification of the models is carried out with the results of the simulations, considering the accuracy, sensitivity, specificity, and execution time of the technique as important parameters of the analysis. Tables 1 and 2 show the best values obtained for accuracy, sensitivity, and specificity according to each of the techniques used. For each value found, the execution time of the respective DM technique is associated.

Table 1. DM1 – hospitalization result.

DM technique	Scenario	Sampling method	Accuracy	Time	Sensitivity	Time	Specificity	Time
JRIP	S5	Cross-validation	91.4	0.00	91.1	0.00	78.9	0.00
J48	S2	Cross-validation	89.2	0.06	89.3	0.06		
	S5	Percentage split					88.6	0.00
RandomForest	S1	Cross-validation	97.8	0.49	98.1	0.49	99.8	0.49
SMO	S1	Cross-validation	91.4	0.2	90.6	0.20		
	S1	Percentage split					71.3	0.16
NaiveBayes	S1	Cross-validation	95.7	0.02	95.7	0.02	89.3	0.02

Table 2. DM2 – surgery complications.

DM technique	Scenario	Sampling method	Accuracy	Time	Sensitivity	Time	Specificity	Time
JRIP	S5	Cross-validation	72.6	0.00				
	S2, S5	Percentage split			83.3	0.00		
	S2, S4	Cross-validation					26.7	0.00
J48	S5	Percentage split	83.2	0.00			64.0	0.00
	S2, S4	Percentage split			83.3	0.01		
RandomForest	S5	Percentage split	82.1	0.01	83.3	0.01	48.7	0.01
SMO	S1	Percentage split	69.0	0.00				
	S2, S3, S4, S5	Percentage split			83.3	0.01		
	S1	Cross-validation					35.9	0.00
NaiveBayes	S1	Percentage split	82.1	0.00				
	S2, S3, S4, S5	Percentage split			83.3	0.00		
	S1	Percentage split					48.7	0.00

As seen from the tables above, there are methods that provide high accuracy results that can be used for future work. In general, it is observed that the execution times of the algorithms are low, and the values of accuracy are high.

4   Discussion

From the analysis of Tables 1 and 2, it is observed that the results of DM1 present values of accuracy, sensitivity, and specificity higher than those of DM2. This worse result is possible associated with the considered attributes that may not have a great influence on the postoperative complications. Another of the differences between DM1 and DM2 is related to the method that presents better results in the classification. In DM1, cross-validation yields better results whereas in DM2 it is the percentage split that has the best results. Regarding the selected scenarios, S1 and S5 have a high predictive character in DM1 and scenarios S2, S4, and S5 are practically equivalent and yield better results in DM2. It should be noted that in DM2, with scenario S2, that only has the attribute "sex" and the classification attribute, it is possible to obtain good values of predictive capacity. However, using, for example, JRIP, the returned rule is simply "no complications", without being associated with the sex attribute. This result indicates that this scenario is not suitable for the intended objectives. The RF and NB techniques present values above 95% in accuracy and sensitivity when used with sample S1, through the cross-validation method for DM1 analysis. Thus, these techniques are the most suitable to be used for DM because they present the best values. Between RF and NB techniques, there is one fundamental difference: RF is much slower in its execution, which can have considerable effects on processing datasets with thousands of instances. It can still be observed that the values of specificity are low in DM2, which removes credibility to these results. Despite this, DM2 presents good values for accuracy and sensitivity, especially when using the sample S5 and the J48, RF or NB techniques.

5 Conclusions and Future Work

In conclusion, it was verified that the dataset of DM1 produced good results for the construction of predictive models, at the level of gastric cancer surgeries. In this case, the RF technique and the cross-validation method should be used. On the other hand, it was also found that not all data allow to obtain good results and that, therefore, they should be reanalysed, such as the DM2 data. Thus, it can be concluded that the RF and NB algorithms are good options in the detection of the result of hospitalization from the clinical data of the patient and that the algorithms J48, RF, and NB offer good predictions for the existence of postoperative complications. To complement the developed work, a new study could be done, with a larger dataset and a bigger number of instances, in order to determine if the results would be maintained for the RF and NB techniques and if the execution time associated with these algorithms would be acceptable.

Acknowledgments. This work has been supported by Compete: POCI-01-0145-FEDER-007043 and FCT within the Project Scope UID/CEC/00319/2013.

References

1. Biglarian, A., Hajizadeh, E., Kazemnejad, A., Zali, M.R.: Application of artificial neural network in predicting the survival rate of gastric cancer patients. Iran. J. Public Health **40**(2), 80–86 (2011)
2. Rugge, M., Fassan, M., Graham, D.Y.: Epidemiology of gastric cancer. In: Strong, V. (ed.) Gastric Cancer, pp. 23–34. Cham, Springer (2015). https://doi.org/10.1007/978-3-319-15826-6_2
3. Brenner, H., Rothenbacher, D., Arndt, V.: Epidemiology of stomach cancer. In: Verma, M. (ed.) Methods of Molecular Biology, pp. 467–477. Springer, Heidelberg (2009). https://doi.org/10.1007/978-1-60327-492-0_23
4. Sitarz, R., Skierucha, M., Mielko, J., Offerhaus, G.J.A., Maciejewski, R., Polkowski, W.: Gastri cancer: epidemiology, prevention, classification, and treatment. Cancer Manag. Res. **10**, 239–248 (2018)
5. Roder, D.M.: The epidemiology of gastric cancer. Gastric Cancer **5**(Suppl 1), 5–11 (2002)
6. Karimi, P., Islami, F., Anandasabapathy, S., Freedman, N.D., Kamangar, F.: Gastric cancer: descriptive epidemiology, risk factors, screening, and prevention. Cancer Epidemiol. Biomark. Prev. **23**(5), 700–713 (2014)
7. Koh, H.C., Tan, G.: Data mining applications in healthcare. J. Healthc. Inf. Manag. **19**(2), 64–72 (2011)
8. Witten, I., Frank, E.: Data Mining: Practical Machine Learning Tools and Techniques, 2nd edn. Morgan Kaufmann, San Francisco (2005)
9. Tuffery, S.: Data Mining and Statistics for Decision-Making, 1st edn. Wiley, Oxford (2011)

10. Fonseca, F., Peixoto, H., Miranda, F., Machado, J., Abelha, A.: Step towards prediction of perineal tear. Procedia Comput. Sci. **113**, 565–570 (2017)
11. Bâra, A., Lungu, I.: Improving decision support systems with data mining techniques. In: Advances in Data Mining Knowledge Discovery and Applications. INTECH Open Access Publisher, pp. 397–418 (2012)
12. Shim, J., Warkentin, M., Courtney, J., Power, D., Sharda, R., Carlsson, C.: Past, present, and future of decision support technology. Decis. Support Syst. **33**(2), 111–126 (2002)
13. Beeler, P., Bates, D., Hug, B.: Clinical decision support systems. Swiss Med. Wkly **144**, w14073 (2014)
14. Trowbridge, R., Weingarten, S.: Clinical decision support systems [Internet], Chap. 53. United States Department of Health & Human Services Agency for Healthcare Research and Quality (2001). https://archive.ahrq.gov/clinic/ptsafety/chap53.htm. Accessed 6 May 2018
15. Morais, A., Peixoto, H., Coimbra, C., Abelha, A., Machado, J.: Predicting the need of Neonatal Resuscitation using data mining. Procedia Comput. Sci. **113**, 571–576 (2017)
16. Svetnik, V., Liaw, A., Tong, C., Culberson, J., Sheridan, R., Feuston, B.: Random forest: a classification and regression tool for compound classification and QSAR modeling. J. Chem. Inf. Comput. Sci. **43**(6), 1947–1958 (2003)
17. Chen, C., Liaw, A., Breiman, L.: Using random forest to learn imbalanced data (2004)
18. Zhang, C., Liu, C., Zhang, X., Almpanidis, G.: An up-to-date comparison of state-of-the-art classification algorithms. Expert Syst. Appl. **82**, 128–150 (2017)
19. Khoshgoftaar, T., Golawala, M., Hulse, J.: An empirical study of learning from imbalanced data using random forest. In: 19th IEEE International Conference on Tools with Artificial Intelligence (ICTAI 2007) (2007)
20. Mitchell, T.: Machine Learning. McGraw-Hill, New York (1997)
21. Platt, J.: Sequential minimal optimization: a fast algorithm for training support vector machines (1998)
22. Wu, X., et al.: Top 10 algorithms in data mining. Knowl. Inf. Syst. **14**(1), 1–37 (2009)
23. Zhao, Y., Zhang, Y.: Comparison of decision tree methods for finding active objects. Adv. Space Res. **41**(12), 1955–1959 (2008)
24. Rajput, A., Aharwal, R., Dubey, M., Saxena, S., Raghuvanshi, M.: J48 and JRIP rules for e-governance data. Int. J. Comput. Sci. Secur. (IJCSS) **5**(2), 201–207 (2011)
25. Mohamed, W., Salleh, M., Omar, A.: A comparative study of reduced error pruning method in decision tree algorithms. In: 2012 IEEE International Conference on Control System, Computing and Engineering, pp. 392–397 (2012)
26. Delen, D., Walker, G., Kadam, A.: Predicting breast cancer survivability: a comparison of three data mining methods. Artif. Intell. Med. **34**(2), 113–127 (2005)
27. Khalilia, M., Chakraborty, S., Popescu, M.: Predicting disease risks from highly imbalanced data using random forest. BMC Med. Informat. Decis.-Making **11**(1), 51 (2011)

A Many-Valued Empirical Machine for Thyroid Dysfunction Assessment

Sofia Santos[1] , M. Rosário Martins[2] , Henrique Vicente[3,4(✉)] ,
M. Gabriel Barroca[5] , Fernando Calisto[5] , César Gama[5] ,
Jorge Ribeiro[6] , Joana Machado[7] , Liliana Ávidos[8] ,
Nuno Araújo[8] , Almeida Dias[8] , and José Neves[4]

[1] Departamento de Química, Escola de Ciências e Tecnologia,
Universidade de Évora, Évora, Portugal
[2] Departamento de Química, Escola de Ciências e Tecnologia,
Laboratório HERCULES, Universidade de Évora, Évora, Portugal
[3] Departamento de Química, Escola de Ciências e Tecnologia,
Centro de Química de Évora, Universidade de Évora, Évora, Portugal
hvicente@uevora.pt
[4] Centro Algoritmi, Universidade do Minho, Braga, Portugal
jneves@di.uminho.pt
[5] SYNLAB Alentejo, Évora, Portugal
[6] Escola Superior de Tecnologia e Gestão, ARC4DigiT – Applied
Research Center for Digital Transformation,
Instituto Politécnico de Viana do Castelo,
Viana do Castelo, Portugal
[7] Farmácia de Lamações, Braga, Portugal
[8] CESPU, Instituto Universitário de Ciências da Saúde, Gandra, Portugal

Abstract. *Thyroid Dysfunction* is a clinical condition that affects thyroid behaviour and is reported to be the most common in all endocrine disorders. It is a multiple factorial pathology condition due to the high incidence of hypothyroidism and hyperthyroidism, which is becoming a serious health problem requiring a detailed study for early diagnosis and monitoring. Understanding the prevalence and risk factors of thyroid disease can be very useful to identify patients for screening and/or follow-up and to minimize their collateral effects. Thus, this paper describes the development of a decision support system that aims to help physicians in the decision-making process regarding thyroid dysfunction assessment. The proposed problem-solving method is based on a symbolic/sub-symbolic line of logical formalisms that have been articulated as an *Artificial Neural Network* approach to data processing, complemented by an unusual approach to *Knowledge Representation and Argumentation* that takes into account the data elements entropic states. The model performs well in the thyroid dysfunction assessment with an accuracy ranging between 93.2% and 96.9%.

Keywords: Thyroid dysfunction · Knowledge Representation and Reasoning ·
Artificial Neural Networks · Entropy · Logic Programming ·
Many-Valued Empirical Machine

1 Introduction

Thyroid is an endocrine gland that produces *Tri-iodothyronine (T3)*, *Thyroxine (T4)* and *Calcitonin*. The *Thyroid Stimulating Hormone (TSH)*, released by pituitary gland, controls the thyroid secretion [1]. Thyroid hormones play a key role in most tissues, including maintenance of cognitive, cardiovascular, bone healthiness, metabolism and body energy balance functions [2]. Main representative thyroid diseases include hypothyroidism, hyperthyroidism, goiter, and autoimmune diseases such as Hashimoto's thyroiditis or Graves' disease, and thyroid cancer [3].

Thyroid Dysfunctions (TDs) are the most common of all endocrine disorders. On average, about 30% to 40% of TD patients are silent and affect more than one million Portuguese and 300 million people worldwide [4, 5]. About 11% of Europeans have *TDs* and only 50% are aware of their condition [5]. The causes of *TDs* are diverse and often associated with genetic factors and iodine levels that play an important role in thyroid hormone regulation, often with a geographical pattern [1]. *TDs* have a higher incidence in female individuals aged 20–75 years old, a tendency that increases with age [5]. *Nutrition* also affects *TDs*, namely legumes such as cabbage, cauliflower, broccoli, goitrogens and soy enriched feed, once reduce *T4* absorption [6]. Thyroid function can also be influenced by green tea high doses intake [7]. Thyroid pathologies quickly change the patient's emotional state, which can be overactive, with anxiety or underactive, with depression. Sleep disorders with poor concentration and short-term memory can occur, most commonly with hypofunction of the thyroid gland. These disorders can cause differences in appearance, such as weight gain or weight loss that may affect self-esteem [1, 3]. Other risk factors may include race differences, cigarette smoking or ambient temperature, namely cold weather, just to name a few [8].

The development of decision support systems for predicting, analyzing and evaluating *TDs* may be an asset to medical personnel, particularly in order to define the finest type of treatment. Such systems are based on features derived from parameters of thyroid markers according to a series of historical data that fed a Proof Theoretical problem-solving line [9], leading to real procedures that pass through *Artificial Neural Networks (ANNs)* approaches to computing [10, 11]. Thus, the present work describes the development of a decision support system that aims to assess the thyroid dysfunction and help physicians in the decision-making process. Behind a technical component, (e.g., issues related with symptomatology, risk factors and the levels of the thyroid biomarkers) such system also includes the behavioral and the psychological dimensions. It is grounded on a *Logic Programming (LP)* approach to *Knowledge Representation* and *Reasoning (KRR)* [9], and complemented by a computer framework centered on *Artificial Neural Networks (ANNs)*.

The article is divided into four sections. The former one defines the goals and the context of the work, followed by a section where one's approach to *KRR* is the object of attention. The next section presents the case study and a possible solution to the problem using *ANNs*. Finally, a conclusion is set and guidelines for future work are outlined.

2 Theoretical Fundamentals

2.1 Knowledge Representation and Reasoning

Knowledge Representation and Reasoning aims to understand the complexity of the information and the associated inference mechanisms. In this study, a data item is to be understood to be slightly smaller in the interior, when it disassembles something, i.e., it is formed mainly of different elements, namely its *Entropic State Range (ESR)*, *ESR's Quality-of-Information (QoI)*, *Degree-of-Confidence (DoC)* that the unknown *Entropic State Value (ESV)* fits into the *ESR*, and the *ESR Potential of Empowerment (PE)*. These are just a set of over an endless item number. It is put in terms of a set of predicates that elicit the universe of discourse, whose extensions are given as productions of the type, viz.

{

$$\neg\, p \leftarrow not\ p, not\ exception_p$$

$$p \leftarrow p_1, \cdots, p_n, not\ q_1, \cdots, not\ q_m$$

$$?\,(p_1, \cdots, p_n, not\ q_1, \cdots, not\ q_m)\ \ (n, m \geq 0)$$

$$exception_{p_1}, \quad \cdots \quad , exception_{p_j}\ \ (0 \leq j \leq k),\ \ being\ k\ an\ integer\ number$$

} :: *entropic state*

where the p_s and q_s are makings of the kind, viz.

$$predicate_{1 \leq i \leq n} - \bigwedge_{1 \leq j \leq m} clause_j \left(\left(\left[ES_{x_1}, ES_{y_1} \right] (QoI_{ESR}, DoC_{ESR}, PE_{ESR}) \right), \cdots \right.$$

$$\left. \cdots , \left(\left[ES_{x_m}, ES_{y_m} \right] (QoI_{ESR}, DoC_{ESR}, PE_{ESR}) \right) \right) :: QoI_j :: DoC_j :: PE_j$$

where n, Λ and m stand for, respectively, the cardinality of the predicates' set, logical conjunction, and predicate's extension cardinality. The items $\left[ES_{x_m}, ES_{y_m} \right]$, QoI_{x_m}, DoC_{x_m} and PE_{x_m} show the way to data item dissection [12, 13], i.e., a data item is to be understood as having an atomic structure. It consists of identifying not only all the sub items that make up an item, but also to investigate the rules that oversee them, i.e., how $\left[ES_{x_m}, ES_{y_m} \right]$, QoI_{x_m}, DoC_{x_m} and PE_{x_m} are kept together and how much added value is therefore created. Indeed, the *ESR* stands for a measure of the unavailable energy in a closed thermodynamic system, i.e., a process of degradation, running down or a trend to disorder, and is given by dark colored areas in Fig. 1. Areas with a gray color indicate a relaxation in the central values, i.e., the corresponding energy values may or may not have been spent. Finally, the *PE* is given by the white areas, and represents an energetic potential that may be available.

2.2 Assessing a Qualitative Data Item in Terms of Its Quantitative Counterpart

In present study both qualitative and quantitative data are present. Taking as an example a set of *3* issues regarding a particular subject, where there are *3* possible options (e.g., *low · medium · high*), which are itemized as a unitary area circle split into 3 (three) slices, being the marks in the axis resembling each of the possible options, viz (Fig. 1).

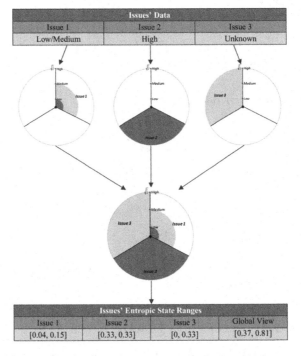

Fig. 1. Going from Qualitative to Quantitative data items.

2.3 Artificial Neural Networks

When one looks to new approaches to problem solving, namely those borrowed from the *Artificial Intelligence* arena which have proven their ability and applicability in terms of prediction, simulation and modeling of physical phenomena, one comes to *ANNs* [11]. *ANNs* are able to capture the embedded spatial and unsteady behavior in the investigated problem, using its architecture and nonlinearity nature, when compared with the other classical problem-solving techniques [10]. Indeed, several decision support systems based on *ANNs* have been applied to various problems in the medical field, namely in cardiovascular diseases, cancer, diabetes or Alzheimer, just to name a few [12–14].

3 Case Study

3.1 Data Collection

The knowledge base includes 354 patients aged between 17 to 98 years old, with an average of 57 ± 17 years old. The gender distribution was 26.6% and 73.4% for male and female, respectively. It was observed that 7% of the population presented a clinical picture suggestive of *TDs*. The parameters of the thyroid markers used in this study were obtained at the SYNLAB-Évora laboratory from June 1st to December 31st, 2017.

The dataset holds information about the factors considered critical in the prediction of *TDs*. These variables were grouped into three takes on, i.e., *Technical*, *Behavioral* and *Psychological* components. The former component considers thyroid biomarkers levels, clinical condition of the patient and relevant risk factors. The second includes issues linked to patients' routines (e.g., dietary and lifestyle) as well as the response to the therapy. Finally, the psychological component comprises mental and emotional features related with the disease and/or treatment.

The Technical Component. This component gathers information related with *Risk Factors*, *Thyroid Biomarkers* and *Symptomatology* (Fig. 2). The issues related with *Risk Factors*, *Thyroid Biomarkers Levels* and *Symptomatology* were valuated according to the scales *low · medium · high*; *normal · abnormal*; and *none · scarcely · sometimes · often*, respectively (Fig. 2).

The evaluation of the $\left[ES_{x_m}, ES_{y_m}\right]$, QoI_{x_m}, DoC_{x_m} and PE_{x_m} parameters to each patient, in terms of the p_s and q_s (Sect. 2.1), is illustrated in Fig. 3 to *patient # 1* for the argument *Sweating* of the relation *Symptomatology*.

The Behavioral Component. This component includes issues regarding *Lifestyle*, *Adherence to Treatment* and *Dietary* (Fig. 4). The items related with *Lifestyle* and *Dietary* were valuated according to the scale *none · scarcely · sometimes · often*, while the scale used to evaluate the *Thyroid Biomarkers Levels* were *low · medium · high* (Fig. 4). The evaluation of the $\left[ES_{x_m}, ES_{y_m}\right]$, QoI_{x_m}, DoC_{x_m} and PE_{x_m} parameters to each patient followed the procedures described above.

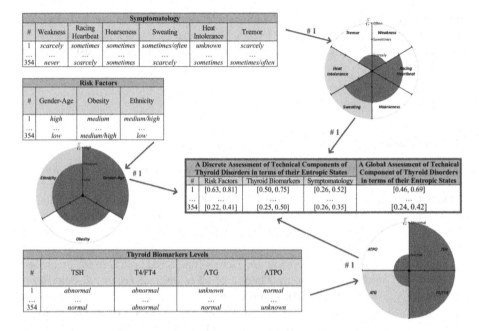

Fig. 2. The extension of the knowledge base for *Technical Component*.

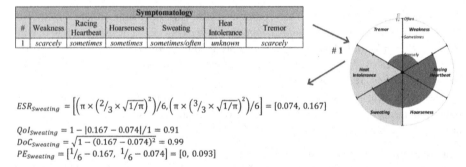

$$ESR_{Sweating} = \left[\left(\pi \times \left(^2/_3 \times \sqrt{1/\pi}\right)^2\right)/6, \left(\pi \times \left(^3/_3 \times \sqrt{1/\pi}\right)^2\right)/6\right] = [0.074, 0.167]$$

$$QoI_{Sweating} = 1 - |0.167 - 0.074|/1 = 0.91$$
$$DoC_{Sweating} = \sqrt{1 - (0.167 - 0.074)^2} = 0.99$$
$$PE_{Sweating} = [^1/_6 - 0.167, \ ^1/_6 - 0.074] = [0, 0.093]$$

Fig. 3. Evaluation of ESR_{x_m}, QoI_{x_m}, DoC_{x_m} and PE_{x_m} parameters to *patient # 1* for the argument *Sweating* of the relation *Symptomatology*.

The Psychological Component. This component comprises psychological features related with *Mental Problems*, *Self-Esteem Damage* and *Emotional Disorders*. *Emotional Disorders* and *Mental Problems* were valuated according to the scale *none · scarcely · sometimes · often*, while the items regarding *Self-Esteem Damage* were valuated according to the scale *low · medium · high* (Fig. 5). As previously, the $\left[ES_{x_m}, ES_{y_m}\right]$, QoI_{x_m}, DoC_{x_m} and PE_{x_m} parameters were evaluated in the same way.

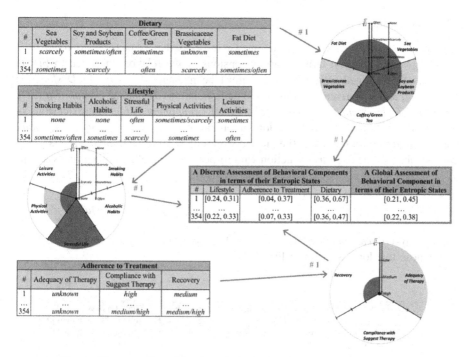

Fig. 4. The extension of the knowledge base for *Behavioral Component*.

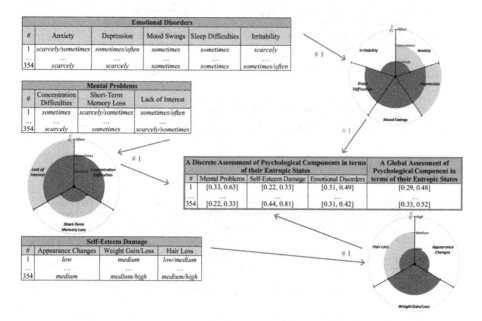

Fig. 5. The extension of the knowledge base for *Psychological Component*.

3.2   Knowledge Base

After being shown how the information was processed it is possible to build up a knowledge base given in terms of the extensions of the relations depicted in Fig. 6. This dataset contained information that must be managed for *Thyroid Dysfunction Assessment*, and it is given in terms of the tables/relations *Technical Component* (*TC*), *Behavioral Component* (*BC*) and *Psychological Component* (*PC*). The extensions of these relations turn into the definition of predicate t_{hyroid} $d_{ysfunction}$ $a_{ssessment}$ (*tda*), which is used to train the *ANNs* (i.e., it will work out *Thyroid Dysfunction Assessment*) and also denotes the objective function with respect to the problem under analyze, viz.

$$tda : T_{echnical}C_{omponent}, \ B_{ehavioral}C_{omponent},$$
$$P_{sychological}C_{omponent} \rightarrow \{true, \ false\}$$

i.e., a *Many-Valued Empirical Machine* for *TDs* assessment is now set in terms of an *ANN* whose topology is given in Fig. 7.

A Discrete Assessment of Psychological Components in terms of their Entropic States			A Global Assessment of Psychological Component in terms of their Entropic States
#	Mental Problems	Self-Esteem Damage	Emotional Disorders	
1	[0.33, 0.63]	[0.22, 0.33]	[0.31, 0.49]	[0.29, 0.48]
... 354	... [0.22, 0.33]	... [0.44, 0.81]	... [0.31, 0.42]	... [0.33, 0.52]

A Discrete Assessment of Behavioral Components in terms of their Entropic States			A Global Assessment of Behavioral Component in terms of their Entropic States
#	Lifestyle	Adherence to Treatment	Dietary	
1	[0.24, 0.31]	[0.04, 0.37]	[0.36, 0.67]	[0.21, 0.45]
... 354	[0.22, 0.33]	... [0.07, 0.33]	... [0.36, 0.47]	... [0.22, 0.38]

Thyroid Dysfunction Assessment in terms of their Entropic States		
#	Technical Component	Behavioral Component	Psychological Component
1	[0.46, 0.69]	[0.21, 0.45]	[0.29, 0.48]
... 354	... [0.24, 0.42]	... [0.22, 0.38]	... [0.33, 0.52]

A Discrete Assessment of Technical Components of Thyroid Disorders in terms of their Entropic States			A Global Assessment of Technical Component of Thyroid Disorders in terms of their Entropic States
#	Risk Factors	Thyroid Biomarkers	Symptomatology	
1	[0.63, 0.81]	[0.50, 0.75]	[0.26, 0.52]	[0.46, 0.69]
... 354	... [0.22, 0.41]	... [0.25, 0.50]	... [0.26, 0.35]	... [0.24, 0.42]

Fig. 6. The thyroid dysfunction assessment's knowledge base.

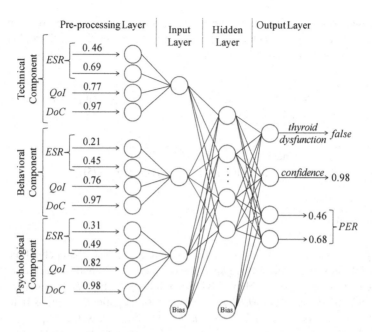

Fig. 7. The *ANN* topology for thyroid dysfunction assessment.

3.3   Computational Model

ANNs were selected due to their dynamic properties such as adaptability, robustness and flexibility. Figure 7 shows how the *ESR*, *ESR's QoI* and *ESR's DoC* values operate as inputs to the *ANN*. The result is the *TDs* assessment as well as a measure of the trust that can be expected from such a prediction and the correspondent *Potential of Empowerment Range* (*PER*).

A set with 354 records were used. The dataset was divided in exclusive subsets through the ten-folds cross validation. In order to guarantee the statistical significance of the attained results 30 (thirty) experiments were applied in all tests. The back-propagation algorithm [15] was used in the learning process of the *ANN*. In the pre-processing layer it was used as activation function the *linear one* (i.e., activation is proportional to input), in the remaining layers the *sigmoid* (i.e., the output of the activation function is going to be in the range [0, 1]; it would not blow up the activations).

Table 1 shows the confusion matrix (the values presented refer to the results obtained in the 30 experiments) for the proposed model. A perusal of Table 1 shows that the model correctly classified [330, 343] of a total of 354 cases, with an accuracy ranging between 93.2% and 96.9%. The values of *Sensitivity*, *Specificity*, *Positive Predictive Value* (*PPV*) and *Negative Predictive Value* (*NPV*) were computed based on the values exhibited in Table 1 [16], presenting a percent in the intervals [93.6, 97.1], [92.8, 96.7], [92.6, 96.9] and [93.9, 97.2], respectively. Such results seem to suggest that the *ANN* model performs well in the thyroid dysfunction assessment. In fact, the inclusion of the *Behavioral* and *Psychological Components* add an essential feature to the proposed model, since some studies point out that such issues (e.g., nutrition, emotional state of patient, mental diseases) can affect the secretion of thyroid hormones and the evolution of *TDs* [1, 6].

Table 1. The confusion matrix regarding proposed model.

Output	Model output	
	True (1)	False (0)
True (1)	TP = [162, 168]	FN = [5, 11]
False (0)	FP = [6, 13]	TN = [168, 175]

4   Conclusions

The early diagnosis of thyroid dysfunction is mandatory to establish patient medication to reverse the disorder. Thus, this paper present a syntheses and characterization of a workable methodology for problem solving that allows for the *TDs* assessment was set as a *Many-Valued Empirical Machine*, i.e., it returns a patient's diagnostic to thyroid dysfunction in terms of a *Truth Value Valuation*. In other words, the proposed approach beyond allowing to obtain the *TDs* diagnosis, also estimate the confidence associated with this finding (98.0% for the example presented above). It must be noted that the word *Empirical* means *based on, concerned with*, or *verifiable by observation or experience* rather than theory or pure logic. The model accuracy, sensibility and sensitivity exhibit percentages ranging in the intervals [93.2, 96.9], [93.6, 97.1], and [92.8, 96.7], respectively. In addition, the paper focuses on the uncertainty measures of proposed epitome, i.e., axiomatic definitions for *ESR*, *QoI*, *DoC*, and *PE* were presented. In upcoming work, we intend to move from *Empirical* to *Logic Machines*, showing the way to *Many-Valued Logic Machines* [17].

Acknowledgments. This work has been supported by COMPETE: POCI-01-0145-FEDER-007043 and FCT – Fundação para a Ciência e Tecnologia within the Project Scope: UID/CEC/00319/2013.

References

1. Imam, S.K., Ahmad, S.I.: Thyroid Disorders. Basic Science and Clinical Practice. Springer, Cham (2016). https://doi.org/10.1007/978-3-319-25871-3
2. Panicker, P.: Genetics of thyroid function and disease. Clin. Biochem. Rev. **32**, 165–175 (2011)
3. Gessl, A., Lemmens-Gruber, R., Kautzky-Willer, A.: Thyroid disorders. In: Regitz-Zagrosek, V. (ed.) Sex and Gender Differences in Pharmacology, Handbook of Experimental Pharmacology, vol. 214, pp. 361–386. Springer, Heidelberg (2013). https://doi.org/10.1007/978-3-642-30726-3_17
4. Garber, J.R., et al.: Clinical practice guidelines for hypothyroidism in adults. Endocr. Pract. **18**(6), 988–1028 (2012)

5. Madariaga, A.G., Palacios, S.S., Guillén-Grima, F., Galofré, J.C.: The incidence and prevalence of thyroid dysfunction in Europe: a meta-analysis. J. Clin. Endocrinol. Metab. **99** (3), 923–931 (2014)
6. Kopp, W.: Nutrition, evaluation and thyroid hormone levels – a link to iodine deficiency disorders? Med. Hypotheses **62**, 871–875 (2004)
7. Chandra, A.K., De, N.: Goitrogenic/antithyroidal potential of green tea extract in relation to catechin in rats. Food Chem. Toxicol. **48**, 2304–2311 (2010)
8. Surks, M.I., Hollowell, J.G.: Age-specific distribution of serum thyrotropin and antithyroid antibodies in the US population: implications for the prevalence of subclinical hypothyroidism. J. Clin. Endocrinol. Metab. **92**, 4575–4582 (2007)
9. Neves, J.: A logic interpreter to handle time and negation in logic databases. In: Muller, R., Pottmyer, J. (eds.) Proceedings of the 1984 Annual Conference of the ACM on the 5th Generation Challenge, pp. 50–54. ACM, New York (1984)
10. Haykin, S.: Neural Networks and Learning Machines, 3rd edn. Prentice Hall, New York (2009)
11. Rocha, M., Cortez, P., Neves, J.: Evolving time séries forecasting ARMA models. J. Heuristics **10**(4), 415–429 (2004)
12. Fernandes, F., Vicente, H., Abelha, A., Machado, J., Novais, P., Neves J.: Artificial neural networks in diabetes control. In: Proceedings of the 2015 Science and Information Conference (SAI 2015), pp. 362–370. IEEE Edition (2015)
13. Ramalhosa, I., et al.: Diagnosis of Alzheimer disease through an artificial neural network based system. In: Cassenti, D.N. (ed.) AHFE 2017. AISC, vol. 591, pp. 162–174. Springer, Cham (2018). https://doi.org/10.1007/978-3-319-60591-3_15
14. Amato, F., López, A., Peña-Méndez, E.M., Vaňhara, P., Hampl, A., Havel, J.: Artificial neural networks in medical diagnosis. J. Appl. Biomed. **11**, 47–58 (2013)
15. Rumelhart, D.E., Hinton, G.E., Williams, R.J.: Learning representations by backpropagating errors. Nature **323**, 533–536 (1986)
16. Vilhena, J., et al.: A case-based reasoning view of thrombophilia risk. J. Biomed. Inform. **62**, 265–275 (2016)
17. Fernandes, B., Vicente, H., Ribeiro, J., Analide, C., Neves, J.: Evolutionary computation on road safety. In: Cassenti, D.N. (ed.) HAIS 2018. LNCS, vol. 10870, pp. 647–657. Springer, Cham (2018). https://doi.org/10.1007/978-3-319-92639-1_54

Detecting Automatic Patterns of Stroke Through Text Mining

Miguel Vieira, Filipe Portela$^{(\boxtimes)}$, and Manuel Filipe Santos

Algoritmi Research Center, University of Minho, Guimarães, Portugal
{cfp,mfs}@dsi.uminho.pt

Abstract. Despite the volume increase of electronic data collection in the health area, there is still much medical information that is recorded without any systematic pattern. For instance, besides the structured admission notes format, there are free text fields for clinicians' patient evaluation observation. Intelligent Decisions Support Systems can benefit from cross-referencing and interpretation of these documents. In the Intensive Care Units, several patients are admitted daily, and several discharge notes are written. To support real-time decision-making and to increase the quality of its process, is crucial to have all relevant patient clinical data available. Since there is no writing pattern followed by all medical doctors, its analysis becomes quite difficult to do. This project aims to make qualitatively and quantitatively analysis of clinical information focusing on the stroke or cerebrovascular accident diagnosis using text analysis tools, namely Natural Language Processing and Text Mining. Our results revealed a set of related words in the clinician' patient diaries that can reveal patterns.

Keywords: Medical information · Admission notes ·
Intelligent Decisions Support Systems · Intensive Care Units

1 Introduction

The medical history of patients is typically documented in clinical notes that are stored in the Electronic Medical Records of the respective healthcare organisation, and contain information about admission, diagnosis, laboratory examination results, potential operations, medication, among others. Clinicians write these notes without following a specific writing pattern, constituting unstructured text that difficult information retrieval. Currently, there are computational tools that enable the analysis of free-text, in different languages. This analysis enables the automatic extraction of valuable information about the patient, which might be ignored. Interestingly, it is possible to find patterns and establish standards for specific clinical events of interest.

The purpose of this article is to analyse unstructured text, finding patterns and thereby facilitating the understanding of the information in such clinical events, in this particular case strokes. Therefore, we have used Natural Language and Text Mining (NLP) algorithms, in order to find patterns and word networks in the admission notes relatively to cerebrovascular accidents. With this type of analysis, the physicians can take decisions more accurately and effectively.

© ICST Institute for Computer Sciences, Social Informatics and Telecommunications Engineering 2019
Published by Springer Nature Switzerland AG 2019. All Rights Reserved
P. Cortez et al. (Eds.): INTETAIN 2018, LNICST 273, pp. 58–67, 2019.
https://doi.org/10.1007/978-3-030-16447-8_6

The Centro Hospitalar Hospital de Santo António provided the dataset, which contains information regarding admission to Intensive Care. This work is divided into four main parts: (i) Background part, where the state of the art is presented; (2) Material and Tools section, which describes the various tools used to elaborate this work, namely an explanation of the KH Coder tool as well as the models that are used; (3) Data Study section for description of data treatment used in this work; (4) Results, Discussion and Future Work sections in which the results of this work are described, as well as its discussion and future work perspectives.

2 Background

2.1 Natural Language Processing

The NLP is a computerised approach based on a set of theories and technologies that allows analysing texts, meaning that computers are used to understand and manipulate the language of a specific text or idiom. An ideal NLP system should be capable of Paraphrase inserted text, translate the text in another type of language, questioning the content of the text, as well as to be capable of deducting about the text [1].

In the medical informatics field, there is a long-time concern with medical language. The data about patients processes are non-numeric and formulated almost exclusively within the constructions of natural language [2]. These constructs were identified as syntactic and semantic constructs origins, becoming important in the development of the Systematic Nomenclature of Multifaceted Pathology (SNOP), later known as SNOMED, and currently SNOMED International (SNOMED III). The possibility of automatic coding pathologies and diagnostic reports in SNOP was a success. Nevertheless, researchers from around the world, such as Canada and the United States, continued to work on the automated indexing of Natural Language clinical reports in SNOMED codes [3]. In 2002 a partnership with SNOMED and CTV3 gave rise to a new version of SNOMED called SNOMED CT. The barrier between the use of different terminologies or international coding systems are smaller, and that data can be presented in various ways, depending the purpose, for example the clinical records presented through SNOMED CT can be processed and presented in different ways, to support direct patient care, clinical audit, research, epidemiology, management and service planning [4].

2.2 Text Mining

Text Mining, also known as Text Data Mining, is a process of extracting useful information patterns from unstructured texts or documents, being an extension of Data Mining. However, is more complicated that Data Mining, since it handles unstructured text data. It brings together a set of various disciplines such as text analysis, information extraction, categorisation, visualisation, database technologies, Machine Learning and Data Mining [5].

Typically, the Text Mining tasks include the following research activities [6]:

- Text categorisation: associate texts to categories;
- Text clustering: groups the texts by categories;
- Sentiment analysis: understand the tone of the text;
- Entity Relational Modelling: summarise the texts and discover relationships between the entities described in the text;

Text Mining, inspired by Data Mining, refers to the process of Knowledge Discovery in Text, known by the acronym KDT. It consists of obtaining information from a natural language text [7]. Knowledge discovery is defined as an implicit and non-trivial extraction of previously unknown data that may be useful. There are two parts regarding Knowledge Discovery; one part consists in the application of statistical analysis techniques and Machine Learning to find patterns on knowledge bases, where the other part focuses on providing them with a guided use for data exploitation [8].

2.3 Admission Notes

An admission note is part of a medical record documenting a patient's condition, including medical history, physical exams, and justification of patient admission to a particular hospital facility, as well as initial instructions to begin patient treatment. Besides these functions, admission note can also have additional notes of the service, progress notes SOAP (Subjective, Objective, Assessment and Plan, this is a method of documentation employed by health care providers), pre-operative, operational, post-operative, procedure and delivery notes, postpartum grades and discharge grades. The admission criteria may vary depending on the area in which the user is admitted. For example, admission in Pediatric Intensive Care is primarily planned for patients without therapeutic limitations, with functional instability of one or more organs requiring monitoring or treatment that cannot be performed outside the CIPE (Pediatric Intensive Care Services) [9].

2.4 Strokes

Approximately 15,5 million cardiovascular deaths occur every day [10]. Strokes are among the leading causes of death and disability in the developed world. In the United States, approximately 500,000 people have a new or recurrent stroke each year. Of these, 150,000 die yearly of stroke [11]. The brain is fully responsible for intelligence, personality, mood and characteristics that individuate us and lead our fellow humans to recognise us as humans. The loss of brain function can be dehumanising, making us dependent on others. Moreover, what could be worse than the sudden inability to speak, to move a limb, to stand, to walk, to see, to read, or to become seriously incapable of understanding spoken language, writing, thinking clearly or not even have the ability to remember things? The Loss of functions is often instantaneous and entirely unpredictable; the damages can be transitory or permanent, mild or devastating [12].

The World Health Organization (WHO) defines a cerebrovascular accident as a focal (or global) neurological impairment that suddenly occurs with symptoms persisting beyond 24 h, or leading to death, with probable vascular origin. Many of the patients who survive have physical, sensory and cognitive sequelae. In a synthesised way, a cerebrovascular accident happens when there is a sudden interruption of cerebral blood flow [12]. Approximately 85% of cerebrovascular accidents are ischemic and 15% haemorrhagic being 10% of intraparenchymal haemorrhage (IPH) and 5% of subarachnoid haemorrhages (SAH).

2.5 Related Work

INTCare is a Clinical Decision Support System (CDSS), based on knowledge discovery in databases (KDD), and on agent-based paradigms with the goal of helping medical decision-making. INTCare is a system that helps clinicians make decisions by detecting patient conditions through continuous updates on their health status and applying the predictive model to predict possible failures that may occur in the next day. INTCare also performs up-to-date maintenance on the probability of death used in an end-of-life decision process. Also, the INTCare also assesses the evolution scenarios of the patient's condition, allowing medical doctors to compare the consequences of different medical procedures [13].

In recent years, several types of evaluations have been developed with the objective of estimating hospital mortality in an ICU. In this study, they predicted one-month mortality related to chronic kidney disease using the Medical Information Mart for Intensive Care III (MIMIC III) database. Also, they observed the improvement in predictive performance and the interpretability of the basic model used in the ICU, for a more complex model using simple resources such as unigrams or bigrams, advanced features, as well as extractions of nursing notes. The primary focus was nursing notes, in which patients who died within the first 24 h of admission and notes that were not updated were excluded. In this study, they observed improvements in the predictive performance and interpretability of predictive models based on new resources extracted from the notes collected in nursing EMRs. More precisely, they predicted one-month mortality at the end of 24 h spent in the ICU in patients with chronic kidney disease (CKD) [14].

3 Material and Tools

3.1 Material Used

The tools used for this work are Microsoft SQL Server 2014, Microsoft Excel, and KH Coder.

3.2 KH Coder

KH Coder is freeware highly utilised for content mining, supporting Japanese, English, French, German, Italian, Portuguese and Spanish etymological information. It works only with .txt files with structured or unstructured text and enables to observe which terms are most used, grouping the terms in the cluster, see the terms frequency and the associations of the word. Individually, it can contribute factual examination co-event system hub structure, computerised arranging guide, multidimensional scaling and comparative calculations [15].

In this work, it will be used some commands through KH coder tool. This analysis was carried out through three models, which are Themes Frequency, Self-Organizational Map and Word Associations. The Themes Frequency model uses an algorithm that can find out which words appear most often in the document and this is done through a function. The function *tf(d, t)* is obtained by dividing the frequency of the word *t* in document *d* by its length, where the length of document *d* is the number of words contained in the document, i.e., the number of morphemes.

$$tf(d, t) = \textit{Frequency of the word t in the document d}/\textit{Length of the document d}.$$
(1)

The Self Organization map enables to explore associations between words through Euclidean distances; the word frequency (adjusted frequency) is standardised before the distance calculation. This ensures the distance of the words is calculated based on occurrence patterns, rather than on whether each word appears frequently or not.

The Word Associations analysis displays a chart where the words closely associated with each other are connected with lines, while words that define the search condition are enclosed in double rectangles. This command enables a way to find words that are closely associated with a specific word, as well as words that are closely associated with a specific code. The possible combinations for the target word are calculated using the Jaccard coefficients [16].

3.3 Dictionary

In order to work with topics of words, a dictionary had to be created for grouping terms into themes which allows a more focused analysis of the document. Anyone can make their own dictionary to analyse the group themes that are related to the project. This dictionary is a group of Portuguese terms that are related to the data, and it was created manually after a deep analysis of the dataset. The purpose of the dictionary is to group words that have the same meaning into topics, making the analysis more accurate and relevant. Without the dictionary, we would have an individual analysis of each word and of words with the same meaning. By grouping the words, the analysis becomes more complete and easier to understand. For example:

*Alteration
alterations | changes | variation | adjustment |
*Negative
no | without | negative |

4 Data Study

The individual patient data used in this analysis were anonymised and provided as part of a partnership with the Hospital Center of Porto, Santo António Hospital.

The dataset has three columns:

- ID: that contains the ID of the patient;
- ENQUADRAMENTO10: the medical history record of the patient, as well as the reasons why the patients are being admitted to the ICU;
- DIAGNÓSTICO: that contains the final patient's diagnosis;

This dataset contains a significant amount of patient's information, so it was needed to treat data, for example deleting all the nulls and extracting only the patient's information with stroke diagnosis. The original dataset has 3363 records, and the dates of these records are between 2010 and April of 2018. The dataset has two types of data format, int and string.

5 Results

Data analysis performed in this work leads to several results. However, it should be noted that these analyses must be interpreted by specialised clinicians, that have the necessary knowledge to make this analysis useful. Using Themes Frequency, that identify the words that appear more frequently in the document, we could observe that the term "artery" appears 45 times, "cerebral" appears 29 times and "right" appear 42 times. With this analysis, we can already have a notion of which are the most important and relevant topics for the study. There is an example of the frequency is presented in Table 1:

Table 1. Frequency topics

Codes	Frequency	Percent
*artery	45	11.45%
*left	34	8.65%
*cerebral	29	7.38%
*right	42	10.69%
*segment	19	4.83%
*thrombus	24	6.11%
*carotid	22	5.60%
*thrombectomy	18	4.58%
*infarct	14	3.56%
*internal	13	3.31%
*cat	19	4.83%
*hemiparesis	13	3.31%
*occlusion	14	3.56%
*hypertension	15	3.82%
*medium	20	5.09%
*neurological	10	2.54%
*admit	0	0.00%
*nihss	12	3.05%
*territory	11	2.80%

(continued)

Table 1. (*continued*)

Codes	Frequency	Percent
*previous	8	2.04%
*stroke	11	2.80%
*basilar	10	2.54%
*catheter	8	2.04%
*distal	10	2.54%
*degree	9	2.29%
*line	0	0.00%
*sedate	0	0.00%
*present	0	0.00%
*arterial	9	2.29%
*eye	8	2.04%

A Self-Organizational Map with six defined clusters presents as follows in Fig. 1:

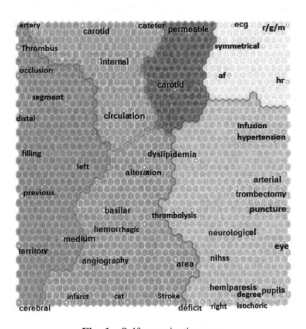

Fig. 1. Self-organization map

Next, we aim to use this command that enables to explore associations between words by creating a self-organising map.

In Fig. 1, it is observed six clusters, and they have several topics inside. The topics are related to the topics inside of the same cluster, and the different colours depicted in the image represent the clusters. This analysis allows to show (through the admission notes where it contains the medical history of all the patients who were hospitalised due to strokes) what were the symptoms responsible for the hospitalisation of the patients in ICU, and thus group them in clusters.

Interestingly, it is possible to verify that there are six different types of patients diagnosed and admitted to the ICU with a cerebrovascular accident. The Self Organization Map can be modified, but in this way, shows a general view of the document:

- In the orange cluster the topics inside are thrombus, occlusion, segment, distal, filling, left, previous, medium, territory and cerebral.
- In the purple cluster, the topics inside are an artery, carotid, internal, circulation and catheter.
- In the blue cluster, the topics inside are an alteration, basilar, haemorrhagic, angiography, area, infarct, computed axial tomography (cat) and stroke.
- In the yellow cluster, the topics inside are permeable and carotid.
- In the green cluster, the topics inside are an infusion, hypertension, dyslipidaemia, arterial, thrombectomy, puncture, neurological, eye, nihss, hemiparesis, degree, deficit, isochoric, right and pupils.
- In the grey cluster, the topics inside are electrocardiogram (ecg), vesicular murmur (r/g/m), symmetrical, arterial fibrillation (af) and heart rate (hr).

If the patient presents a set of symptoms of one of the clusters it is most likely that he or she had a stroke, or it will have in the future, therefore if a patient does not belong to any of these clusters, most likely he has not suffered, or will not suffer from any type of cerebrovascular accident.

A Word Association with the term "artery" presents as follows (Fig. 2):

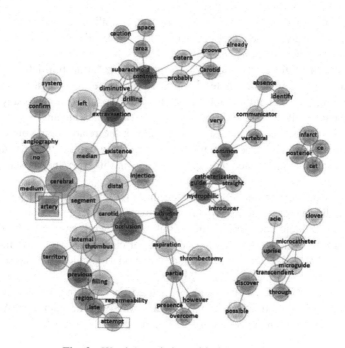

Fig. 2. Word Association with the term artery

Here it can be seen the Word Association, where the chosen word was, "artery" and through that word, it can be seen the network presented in Fig. 2. The chosen word was "artery", because it was the word that appeared most often in the patient's admission notes (as shown in Table 1), thus indicating that it is one of the essential words regarding stroke, since strokes occurs when there is a clogging or rupture of the arteries (arteries of the brain).

That shows the words that are associated with artery term. With this technique, it is possible to discover what are the different types of words that occurred with any term that is chosen. For example, the word artery, in the text, it appears associated many times with cerebral as with carotid because cerebral and carotid are two types of the artery. However, the word cerebral appears connected with the word middle that's because it is also a type of artery, called middle cerebral artery. With this type of analysis is shown associations of any words that appear in the admission notes and obtain relations with other words that could go unnoticed, to discovering new patterns related to strokes.

6 Discussion and Future Work

As shown in the results, through a simple word, or a set of words and their relations several conclusions can be obtained. To this conclusion be more precise and better understood, its necessary to be performed for professionalised people like clinicians with the expert knowledge.

In the first analysis, Table 1, it can be seen what the themes that appear more often are and how they appear in the dataset.

In the second analysis, Fig. 1, it is already seen a qualitative dataset analysis. This analysis enables to divide the terms that occur more frequently by the cluster. As it can be seen in Fig. 1, for example, one of the clusters has the terms "mv" that means vesicular murmurs, "electrocardiogram", "symmetrical", "atrial fibrillation", "hr" that means "heart rate". These are the terms grouped in a type of admission notes for an ICU. Therefore, by the contrary logic, patients who do not belong to any of these clusters, probably will not suffer from any cerebrovascular accident.

In the Word Association analysis, Fig. 2, shows the relationships of words on a specific chosen topic. This type of analysis can be beneficial to see what are the events, or even diseases, that are related to a specific word, in this case, the chosen word was "artery".

With this work, it is possible to conclude that through unstructured text, it can be created and discovered patterns, which can be an advantage to make the clinical decision more accurate and faster. Indeed, this type of work can be adapted to other areas of medicine. This work consisted primarily of choosing a particular information type from a global dataset and the creation of a dictionary to allow the various analysis made.

The future work in this field could be focused on exploring a more general and complex dataset, with more information and with more types of diagnoses. After an in-depth analysis with more information, it will be possible to create models of text mining prediction to automatically predict what the patient may have in the future, for example, diseases.

Acknowledgements. This work has been supported by COMPETE: POCI-01-0145-FEDER-007043 and FCT – Fundação para a Ciência e Tecnologia within the Project Scope: UID/CEC/00319/2013. This work is also supported by the Deus ex Machina (DEM): Symbiotic technology for societal efficiency gains - NORTE-01-0145-FEDER-000026.

References

1. Chowdhury, G.: Natural language processing. Annual Review of this is an author-produced version of a paper published in The Annual Review of Information Science and Technology ISSN 0066–4200. This version has been peer-reviewed, but does not. Annu. Rev. Inf. Sci. Technol. **37**, 51–89 (2003)
2. Aw, P.: Medicine, computers, and linguistics. Adv. Biomed. Eng. **3**, 97–140 (1973)
3. Sager, N., Lyman, M., Bucknall, C., Nhan, N., Tick, L.J.: Natural language processing and the representation of clinical data. J. Am. Med. Inform. Assoc. **1**(2), 142–160 (1994)
4. SNOMED: SNOMED International, no. Dec 2010 (2006)
5. Tan, A.-H.: Text mining: the state of the art and the challenges. In: Proceedings of PAKDD 1999 Workshop on Knowledge Discovery from Advanced Databases, vol. 8, pp. 65–70 (1999)
6. Truyens, M., Van Eecke, P.: Legal aspects of text mining. Comput. Law Secur. Rev. **30**(2), 153–170 (2014)
7. Zhao, Y.: Text mining. In: R Data Mining, pp. 105–122 (2013)
8. Feldman, R., Dagan, I.: Knowledge discovery in textual databases (KDT). In: International Conference on Knowledge Discovery and Data Mining, pp. 112–117 (1995)
9. Pedi, C.I.: Critérios de admissão no Serviço de Cuidados Intensivos Pediátricos. pp. 2–3 (2014)
10. Part I: General Considerations, the Epidemiologic Transition: Clinical Cardiology : New Frontiers Global Burden of Cardiovascular Diseases, no. C (2001)
11. De Magalhães, R., De Oliveira, C., Augusto, L., De Andrade, F.: Artigos Acidente vascular cerebral, vol. 8, no. 3, pp. 280–290 (2001)
12. Alves, C.: Determinantes da capacidade funcional do doente após acidente vascular cerebral (2011)
13. Gago, P., Santos, M.F., Silva, A., Cortez, P., Neves, J., Gomes, L.: INTCare: a knowledge discovery based intelligent decision support system for intensive care medicine. J. Decis. Syst. **14**(3), 241–259 (2005)
14. Kocbek, P., Fijačko, N., Zorman, M., Kocbek, S., Štiglic, G.: Improving mortality prediction for intensive care unit patients using text mining techniques, pp. 2–5 (2012)
15. Gowri, S., Anandha Mala, G.S.: Efficacious IR system for investigation in digital textual data. Indian J. Sci. Technol. **8**(12), 43102 (2015)
16. Higuchi, K.: KH coder. Ref. Man. 99 (2016). http://khcoder.net/en/manual_en_v2.pdf

A Preliminary Evaluation of a Computer Vision-Based System to Detect Effects of Aromatherapy During High School Classes via Movement Analysis

Ksenia Kolykhalova[1]([✉]), David O'Sullivan[2], Stefano Piana[1], Hyungsook Kim[3], Yonghyun Park[3], and Antonio Camurri[1]

[1] Casa-Paganini - InfoMus, DIBRIS, University of Genova, Genova, Italy
ksenia.kolykhalova@dibris.unige.it
[2] Division of Sport Science, Pusan National University, Busan, Republic of Korea
[3] Department of Art Technology, Inha University, Incheon, Republic of Korea

Abstract. In this paper we present a pilot study on non-intrusive visual observation and estimation of affective parameter using recorded videos (RGB). We aim at estimating student engagement analyzing upper-body movement comparing two different classroom settings: with the introduction of aromatherapy during the class vs standard lesson. Following previous studies on how aromatherapy can alter movement behaviour, we chose Lavender essential oil. We used computer vision techniques for pose estimation and developed software modules for the extraction of movement features from media data. Data show significant increases in overall velocity and acceleration when the participants are exposed to the aromatherapy condition. Significant decreases in neck flexion angle has been also observed, that shows students had a straighter head posture (i.e. sitting up straighter). No significant differences were observed for the overall kinetic energy of the joints and spinal extension.

Keywords: Movement analysis · Aromatherapy · Pose estimation

1 Introduction

In this paper we present a pilot study in the framework of Project "Effect of olfactory stimulation on extending concentration behavior patterns in high school students". The main objectives are: (1) investigate the effect of essentials oils on movement behaviour of high school students during the lessons; (2) application of computer vision techniques for data processing and analysis of movement features to detect the effect of aromatherapy. We chose to use Lavender essential oil because of its powerful antioxidant, antimicrobial, calming and anti depressive properties [2]. Four high school students (out of 15 students in the class) were recruited and attended the classes in two different conditions: (i) without and (ii) with exposure to lavender oil (necklace with essential oil).

P. Cortez et al. (Eds.): INTETAIN 2018, LNICST 273, pp. 68–72, 2019.
https://doi.org/10.1007/978-3-030-16447-8_7

Academic life in Korean high schools is very stressful, this influences students that have consequently poor academic performance which is reported to be a major trigger for depression, anxiety, and suicidal intentions [3] and vice-versa [4]. The use of essential oils has been reported in medical studies [5] for various therapeutic methods for treating physical and emotional well-being [6].

Lefter and associates has investigated applying novel methods of measuring stress from human to human interactions and audiovisual recordings [7]. A distinct advantage of methods [7] for measuring stress are the non-invasive measurement technique, which can be applicable in numerous situations. Therefore, we aim to investigate if computer vision techniques applied to video recordings of an actual classroom in high school are feasible to detect differences in movement behaviour. In this study the experimental settings are based on non-intrusive data collection through HD video camera. For post processing of the recorded data we use OpenPose [1] for estimation of position of joints, Matlab for processing positional data and tracking of the subjects, EyesWeb XMI for the extraction of movement features. Finally, we perform statistical analysis on the movement features to see the difference between with and without essential oil lessons.

2   Experimental and Computational Details

2.1   Participants, Testing Procedure and Equipment

The National Universities Institutional Review Board (IRB) approved all procedures for this study. A high school class of 15 students participated in experimental recordings, during an extra-curricular class (subject: Social Studies). 4 of the students volunteered and agreed to be further analyzed in the framework of the study with the consent of the parents. The settings of the experimental recordings were held ecologically, as a usual high school class.

The subjects were studied during two separate days: one day without aromatherapy, and one with lavender aromatherapy. The two conditions were separated by a week of pause. The recorded subjects, teacher and room settings were the same for both days. The duration of the class was 90 min. On the second day of recordings, participants wore a lavender essential oil filled necklace during the whole class. Both classes were recorded with four high definition cameras installed in four different sides of the classroom, adequately covering the required space. Videos were recorded at full-HD (1920×1080) resolution and 100 Frames per second.

2.2   Data Processing

To analyze subjects' movements we used Convolutional Pose Machines (CPM) developed by The Carnegie Mellon University (CMU) [1] for pose estimation (Fig. 1a). CMP is a novel technique, that consists of a deep neural network for estimating articulated poses [1]. We extracted the position of 14 body parts, related to upper-part of the body: nose, neck, right and left shoulders, elbows, wrists, hips, and eyes for each frame see Fig. 1(b). With CPM output we performed tracking and matching of subjects based on the minimum Euclidean distance of the body centroid, taking into account the assumption that people are siting and do not move from their places. In this step, we computed and filtered the positional data of the X, Y coordinated of 14 jointed named previously, for each participant separately. The extracted skeletal data, then is used for calculation of meaningful movement features, from low-level to higher level.

Fig. 1. (a) Application of CMP (b) Locations of 14 joints

2.3 Movement Features Extraction

Considering the limitations of the movements that can be executed during the school, we focused our analysis on upper-body movements. First we extracted low-level motion features at a small time scale (i.e., observable frame-by-frame), such as velocity, acceleration and kinetic energy. We perform the movement feature extraction using EyesWeb XMI[1]. EyesWeb XMI was used to read positional data, generate bi-dimensional points (x, y) for each joint and for the calculation of kinematic values and features. For this preliminary study, we extracted two geometrical features of the upper-body: the spinal extension and neck angle between the head and torso. The straightness of the back of a student is varying during the class, depending on many factors such as: attention, tiredness, focus, interest etc. In order to measure the extension of the back, the distance between the position of the neck and the mid-point of the hips is computed for each given frame. Movements such as look up to the teacher or look down on the book involve the head to be moving up and down, therefore changing the angle between head and torso. To analyze such movements we computed the angle between two vectors: the first connecting the barycenter of the head and the neck, and the second connecting neck and the barycenter of the hips.

---

[1] (http://www.infomus.org/eyesweb_eng.php) is a development software, that supports multimodal analysis and processing of non-verbal expressive gestures.

3   Results

In this preliminary study the overall velocity, acceleration and energy of neck, left and right shoulder, left and right elbow and left and right wrist were analyzed. There were significant differences in the overall acceleration and velocity of upper-body joints between the two conditions: with and without aromatherapy $[F(1, 54) = 4.53, p = 0.037]$ and $[F(1, 54) = 4.10, p = 0.047]$ respectively. However, there was no difference $[F(1, 54) = 1.10, p = 0.32)$ reported for the energy as there were substantially large standard deviations between each of the participants. There was a significant difference between the neck flexion angle between the two conditions $[F(1, 30) = 3.61, p = 0.065]$. However, the spinal extension doesn't differ significantly $[F(1, 30) = 0.50, p = 0.48]$.

4   Discussions and Conclusion

When participants were exposed to lavender essential oil, data shows significant increases in overall velocity and acceleration. Based on detailed observation of the recordings the student's faster moves may be explained as re-engagement of attention on the teacher. A decrease in neck flexion angle was also observed: students had a straighter head posture (i.e. sitting up straighter), which could be indicating that they were paying more attention to the teacher. This study highlights that relatively low cost cameras can provide a sufficient level of quality to use this data for estimating the positions and perform movement analysis of multiple participants in a classroom setting.

In conclusion, this study shows the possibility of using movement qualities, such as kinematic and geometric movement features, extracted ecologically using non-invasive equipment, as a novel method to measure change of movement behaviour due to aromatherapy. Future studies will involve a wider set of movement features and a bigger number of participants.

Acknowledgments. This work was supported by Global Research Network program through the Ministry of Education of the Republic of Korea and the National Research Foundation of Korea [NRF-2016S1A2A2912583].

References

1. Wei, S., Ramakrishna, V., Kanade, T., Sheikh, Y.: Convolutional pose machines. In: IEEE Conference on Computer Vision and Pattern Recognition, pp. 4724–4732 (2006)
2. Cavanagh, H.M., Wilkinson, J.M.: Biological activities of Lavender essential oil. Phytother. Res. **16**, 301–308 (2002). https://doi.org/10.1002/ptr.1103
3. Kim, H., Song, Y.J., Yi, J.J., Chung, W.J., Nam, C.M.: Changes in mortality after the recent economic crisis in South Korea. Ann. Epidemiol. **14**, 442–446 (2004)
4. Lee, M.: Korean adolescents' "examination hell" and their use of free time. New Dir. Child Adolesc. Dev. **99**, 9–22 (2003)
5. Bartram, T.: Encyclopaedia of Herbal Medicines. Grace Publishers, Dorset (1995)

6. PDQ Integrative, Alternative, and Complementary Therapies Editorial Board. https://www.cancer.gov/about-cancer/treatment/cam/patient/cam-topics-pdq. Accessed 20 Sept 2018
7. Lefter, I., Burghouts, G.J., Rothkrantz, L.J.: An audio-visual dataset of human-human interactions in stressful situations. J. Multimodal User Interface 8(1), 29–41 (2014)

Computational Inference Applied to Social Profiling

Virtual Agents for Professional Social Skills Training: An Overview of the State-of-the-Art

Kim Bosman[1], Tibor Bosse[2(✉)], and Daniel Formolo[1]

[1] Department of Computer Science, Vrije Universiteit, Amsterdam, The Netherlands
[2] Behavioural Science Institute, Radboud Universiteit, Nijmegen, The Netherlands
t.bosse@ru.nl

Abstract. Training of interpersonal communication skills is typically done using role play, by practising relevant scenarios with the help of professional actors. However, as a result of the rapid developments in human-computer interaction, there has been an increasing interest in the use of computers for training of social and communicative skills. This type of training offers opportunities to complement traditional training methods with a novel paradigm that is more scalable and cost-effective. The main idea of such applications is that of a simulated conversation between a human trainee and a virtual agent. By developing the system in such a way that the communicative behaviour of the human has a direct impact on the behaviour of the virtual agent, an interactive learning experience is created. In this article, we review the current state-of-the-art in virtual agents for social skills training. We provide an overview of existing applications, and discuss various properties of these applications.

Keywords: Review · Virtual agents · Social skills training · Serious games

1 Introduction

Having good interpersonal communication skills is an important ability for human beings to be able to function in daily life. According to [4], interpersonal communication skills is an umbrella term that covers a number of core competencies, including non-verbal communication, questioning, reinforcement, reflecting, explaining, self-disclosure, listening and humour. Unfortunately, the extent to which people possess these skills varies greatly per individual. The good news is that communication skills can be trained, at least to a certain extent. To enable professionals to practice and improve the social skills they require for their job, organizations invest a lot of time and money into training programs. Traditionally, such training programs make use of role play, through which participants can practice certain simulated scenarios either with professional actors or with teachers or classmates [10,14].

© ICST Institute for Computer Sciences, Social Informatics and Telecommunications Engineering 2019
Published by Springer Nature Switzerland AG 2019. All Rights Reserved
P. Cortez et al. (Eds.): INTETAIN 2018, LNICST 273, pp. 75–84, 2019.
https://doi.org/10.1007/978-3-030-16447-8_8

Although this type of training can be reasonably effective, it suffers from several drawbacks. First, organizing training sessions is very costly, both in terms of money and time. As a result, the frequency by which they are offered is low. Second, there are large differences in the successfulness of role-play-based training: for some students, the learning effect is large, whereas for others it is minimal. And third, training is never fully completed. As argued in [17], employees need frequent refreshing sessions, which often conflict with regular work schedules. In conclusion, existing approaches are hard to tailor to individual needs, and difficult to combine with work schedules.

As a complementary approach to role play, communication skills can be trained via serious games. According to [19], a Serious Game is "a mental contest, played with a computer in accordance with specific rules, that uses entertainment to further government or corporate training, education, health, public policy, and strategic communication objectives". Within the serious games domain, there has been increasing interest in the use of Intelligent Virtual Agents (IVAs) for training of social skills. IVAs can be defined as 'intelligent digital interactive characters that can communicate with humans and other agents using natural human modalities like facial expressions, speech, gestures and movement' [2].

The current article describes a number of representative applications in the area of IVAs for social skills training. The main purpose of this paper is not to describe new research results, nor to provide an exhaustive literature review. Instead, it is meant to provide a high level overview of existing approaches regarding IVAs for social skills training. A representative selection of recent applications is reviewed, and the systems are categorized according to a list of characteristics such as the application domain, the interaction modalities, and the extent to which the system has been evaluated.

2   IVAs for Social Skills Training

IVAs for social skills training are typically part of a larger system that can be called a Virtual Learning Environment. In [7], Virtual Learning Environments are defined as 'a multi-dimensional experience which is totally or partially computer generated and can be accepted by the participant as cognitively valid'. The key idea is that the user's senses are stimulated in such a way that the virtual environment is almost experienced as a real environment. Users or players are considered those who play the a serious game with the deliberate aim of improve the abilities for which the game is proposed.

Over the years, the graphics of virtual environments have become increasingly realistic, mainly due to the developments in the video games and military simulation industry [19]. Moreover, recent developments in Artificial Intelligence have paved the way for virtual environments for social skills training, which is the focus of the current paper.

Social skills are those abilities that people use to communicate with each other, both verbally and non-verbally, and it is important to be able to show the appropriate verbal and non-verbal behaviours. To be able to develop these skills in a simulation-based environment, it is important that the virtual environment closely resembles the real environment. Another important aspect that determines the user's experience is the extent to which the interaction between the user and the IVA is perceived as natural or *believable* [1]. That could be measured through surveys or biofeedback signals monitoring user's body reactions to the IVA's acts. If the virtual characters do not behave like people would normally behave in a particular situation, the credibility of the simulation decreases, which may in turn decrease the learning effect [3]. Other parameters that determine the quality of the experience include the graphics frame rate, the tracking capabilities, tracking latency (the time it takes before a head movement results in the correct change in the display), image quality, the amount of field a user can see, the behaviour of objects, and the range of sensory accommodations [12].

Furthermore, the success of a virtual learning environment depends to a considerable extent on the user's acceptance. As argued in [16], individually tailored e-learning environments will have a higher acceptance rate. Nevertheless, in many cases, e-learning has been found to be just as effective (e.g., [18]), or even more effective [15] than class-based learning.

In order to build IVAs for social skills training, typically a modular approach is taken, where developers first create separate modules for specific capabilities of the agent, and then integrate them into a coherent system. An overview of the various capabilities that an IVA might have, taken from [5], is shown in Fig. 1. This figure shows the possible capabilities of an IVA (represented by the rectangles) and their interactions at an abstract level.

The details of Fig. 1 are beyond the scope of this paper, but a rough summary is as follows. Typically, a human user (lower-left) interacts with a virtual agent of which the behaviour is displayed via a renderer (lower-right). The four rectangles on the left hand side of the figure represent processing of the user's *input*, of which the two modules on the left deal with non-verbal information and the modules on the right with verbal information. Similarly, the four rectangles on the right hand side of the figure are about generating the agent's *output*. Here, the two modules on the right deal with non-verbal information (e.g., displaying facial expressions on the agent's face) and the modules on the left with verbal information (i.e., determining what the agent says). The agent module, shown in the upper part of the picture, is an *internal* layer that connects the input to the output. For instance, a simple way to implement this would be to use a fixed question-answering mechanism that generates pre-defined responses for certain questions asked by the user [9]. However, more complex implementations make use of sophisticated dialogue managers that keep track of the progress of the conversation with the user.

As displayed in Fig. 1, on top of a system another layer is implemented to generate explicit *feedback* (e.g., using computational models of the task and the user's performance [6]). Providing feedback on the performance of the trainee is an important mechanism to facilitate learning. Within the context of IVA-based training, feedback may have the form of hints to inform the trainee that certain behaviour during the simulated scenario was appropriate or inappropriate. In

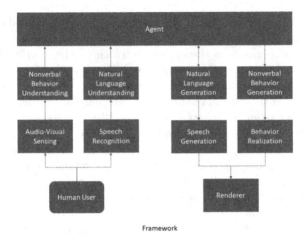

Framework

Fig. 1. ICT virtual agent architecture

addition, it is often claimed that after-session feedback is an effective method to enhance learning [13].

Finally, an important question to be addressed when developing IVA-based systems for social skills training is to what extent they are actually effective in enhancing a person's communication skills? When it comes to evaluation of training interventions, Kirkpatrick's framework is a useful instrument [8]. It distinguishes four evaluation levels, named (1) reaction ('do participants like the training?'), (2) learning ('do participants acquire the intended skills?'), (3) behavior ('do participants apply the learned behavior in practice?'), and (4) results ('does the training result in the targeted outcomes?').

The next sections discuss a number of recent projects involving IVAs for social skills training. First, in Sect. 3, the separate projects are briefly summarized. After that, in Sect. 4, they are compared according to a list of characteristics. The characteristics that are used for the comparison directly follow from the discussion above (and are related to the terms written in italics in the current section), namely: input, output, internal, feedback and evaluation. A sixth characteristic, *formalism*, has been added to provide information about the type of modelling framework or formal representation that has been used (e.g., AIML or Finite State Machines).

3   A Selection of Existing Applications

The search engines *Google Scholar*, *IEEE*, and *ACM library* were used to find relevant articles. Articles from before the year 2000 were not considered. Search terms like *Conversational Agent*, *Virtual Human*, *Virtual Agent* and *Avatar* were used in combination with terms like *Social Skills Training* and *Conversational Skills Training*. This resulted in slightly less than 1000 articles. However, a substantial number of search results turned out to be out of scope, so many of them were disregarded after reading the abstract. The main inclusion criteria were (1) the presence of a visually embodied agent, (2) the aim to train people's social or communicative skills, and (3) the presence of an implemented system. Hence, papers describing purely theoretical models or partially implemented systems were discarded. Also, papers describing commercial applications were excluded because they normally don't provide any details about the implementation of the system. Moreover, this literature study focuses on applications aimed to improve social skills required for professionals in work environments, e.g., in domains like healthcare, education, law enforcement and military. In contrast, it does not cover social skills training in psychotherapeutic context. Hence, also these articles were discarded. For this domain, an extensive review has been conducted by Provoost and colleagues [11].

Table 1. Summary of the twelve applications

Project	Input	Output	Internal
ASST *Decrease discomfort*	Speech	Speech Facial expressions	Scenario engine
Believable Suspect Agents *Police interrogations*	Free text Speech	Speech	Response model based on stance
BiLAT *Cross-cultural negotiations*	Specified menu choices (say, ask, give, do)	Speech Gestures	Rule-based responses
ColCoMa *Conflict management*	Free text	Text Facial expressions	AIML-processor
Communicate! *Communication skills*	Specified menu choices	Emotion Speech	Consultation graphs
deLearyous *Communication skills*	Free text	Pre-recorded audio Visual feedback	Scenario engine using sentiment
INOTS *Counseling*	Specified menu choices Heart rate, EDA	Speech	Conversation trees
MRES *Critical decision-making*	Speech	Speech, Gestures Facial expressions	Focus mechanism via Soar architecture
STRESS *Aggression de-escalation*	Specified menu choices Heart rate, EDA, EEG	Pre-recorded audio Facial expressions Gestures	Conversation trees
Virtual Patient *Medical interviews*	Free text Gestures	Facial expressions Text	AIML-processor
Virtual Recruiter *Job interviews*	Speech Multi-modal cues	Speech	Sequential behaviour planner based on stance
Virtual-Suspect *Police interrogations*	Free text	Text	Scenario engine

Once a relevant paper was found, the references used in this article were checked as well. This resulted in a selection of twelve papers. As the papers describe rather diverse approaches and application domains, we feel that this selection provides a fairly representative overview of the current state-of-the-art. However, we do not claim that this overview is exhaustive. The selected papers have been categorized and compared according to the criteria identified in Sect. 2; see Tables 1 and 2.

Table 2. Summary of the twelve applications (continued)

Project	Feedback	Evaluation	Formalism
ASST *Decrease discomfort*	Hints afterwards Scores	Level 2	MMDAAgent Snak Sound Toolkit
Believable Suspect Agents *Police interrogations*	Mood changes Thought bubbles Final reflection	Level 2	Interpersonal Circumplex NPCEditor
BiLAT *Cross-cultural negotiations*	Reflective tutor State changes	Level 2	PsychSim Intelligent tutoring system
ColCoMa *Conflict management*	Feedback from opponent Textual feedback Replay session	Level 1	AIML-Chatbot Facial animations C# and .NET
Communicate! *Communication skills*	Emotion changes Annotated textual feedback Scored goals	Level 1	Domain reasoner
deLearyous *Communication skills*	Position change	Unknown	NLP Interpersonal Circumplex Finite State Machine
INOTS *Counseling*	After-action review Homework review	Level 2	I-CARE framework LiSA-CARE framework
MRES *Critical decision-making*	Run-time adjustments	Unknown	Multigen-Paradigm's PSERT, DIRM
STRESS *Aggression de-escalation*	Run-time adjustments Hints afterwards	Level 2	InterACT Adaptive training
Virtual Patient *Medical interviews*	Annotated transcript Scores	Level 1	AIML-chatbot HTML, CSS, PHP, JS
Virtual Recruiter *Job interviews*	Mood changes Personality changes	Level 3	SSI Interpersonal Circumplex
Virtual-Suspect *Police interrogations*	After-action review Mood changes	Level 1	Not reported

4   Overview

This section provides an overview of the twelve applications that have been discussed. As mentioned in Sect. 2, the applications are compared according to six characteristics: input, output, internal, feedback, evaluation and formalism. The results are shown in Tables 1 and 2.

As becomes clear from the tables, there is a wide variety in the approaches used to train social skills using IVAs. However, one can also see that some methods are more commonly used than others. Below, these similarities and differences are discussed per characteristic. However, it is important to point out that the papers that were reviewed differed with respect to the level of detail in which the application was described. The comparisons made in the tables are solely based on the information that was available.

4.1 Input

There are roughly three approaches to allow the user to provide verbal input to the system, namely: free speech, free text input, and pre-determined multiple choice options. Obviously, each of these options has its pros and cons. Typically, interacting with an IVA using free speech is perceived as more natural than typing text, or selecting options from a multiple choice menu. In addition, the latter brings along a risk that users feel forced to select answers that they would never give in real life. On the other hand, free speech or text is clearly more difficult to process (on a semantic level) than pre-defined sentences, which increases the risk that the system generates inappropriate responses or 'backup' responses like 'I do not understand, please rephrase'.

Regarding non-verbal input, some systems (e.g. Virtual Recruiter) extract social cues from multi-modal input such as facial expressions or gestures. The purpose of this is to understand not only what is said, but also 'how' the user says something. In addition, INOTS and STRESS take physiological signals like heart rate, EDA or EEG signals into account.

4.2 Output

Also on the level of the output (i.e., the behaviour displayed by the IVA) a distinction can be made between verbal and non-verbal aspects. Regarding verbal aspects, all systems use either text or speech, with the latter being most popular. Speech is either generated based on pre-recorded audio files or is generated at run-time using text-to-speech engines. Non-verbal elements are not used by all systems, but in several cases they are used to enhance the believability of the agents. The non-verbal cues that are used are mostly facial expressions and (less frequently) gestures.

4.3 Internal

To determine how the virtual agent should respond, different methods are available. The trigger for activating these methods is the input from the player (see Sect. 4.1). However, depending on the method, the input is either directly mapped to output, or is first interpreted in terms of higher level intermediate constructs. More advanced systems first try to make an interpretation of the user's (verbal and/or non-verbal) input, for instance in terms of the atmosphere of the conversation (MRES or Virtual Patient), sentiment of the text (deLearyous), or the interpersonal stance that is taken (Believable Suspect Agents or Virtual Recruiter). Subsequently, this intermediate construct is then processed by some agent model. to determine on a high level how the agent should respond. An alternative method is to use markup languages for natural language generation as part of the internal module (ColCoMa or Virtual Patient).

Again, there is a large variety in the approaches that are taken, and there is no clear best approach. The advantage of simple input-output mappings clearly is that they are easy to handle by the developer. However, a drawback is that they may result in agent behaviour that is perceived as static and inflexible. This may be sufficient for some applications , but it is detrimental for others . In such cases, often more complex agent models are used, to allow for a wider variety of IVA behaviour. Another advantage of such complex approaches is that the history of the conversation can be taken into account (e.g., the IVA may still be in a bad mood because of something the user said some time ago), which is impossible with simple input-output mappings.

Finally, it is worth mentioning that almost all of the systems use a 'turn-taking' protocol, where the user is only allowed to provide input after the agent has finished speaking (and vice versa). An exception is ColCoMa, where the interaction between two human players is mediated by a chatbot.

4.4   Feedback

As mentioned earlier, providing feedback on the performance of the trainee is an important mechanism to facilitate learning. In the papers that were reviewed, various forms of feedback were encountered: feedback during the simulation, after the simulation, by a virtual coach, by human instructors, on paper, and via a replay of the simulation. Most of the applications offer either a textual summary (sometimes with notes) or an actual sit-down with a human coach to review the process. Besides these 'after-action reviews', it is also common to adjust the scenario while it is still running. The main idea behind these run-time adjustments is that the player receives immediate feedback on his or her choices during the interaction. For instance, if the learning goal of a system is to show empathy to frustrated customers, the IVA can be implemented in such a way that it calms down if the user takes an empathic stance, but otherwise becomes even more aggressive. This way, the behaviour of the IVA functions as an implicit reward or punishment, hence facilitating a kind of associative learning process.

4.5   Evaluation

The twelve applications are classified on the basis of Kirkpatrick's four levels of evaluation [8]. Most applications have been evaluated on the levels 1 or 2. Based on the information that was available, we categorized ColCoMa, Communicate!, Virtual Patient and Virtual-Suspect into Level 1; ASST, Believable Suspect Agents, BiLAT, INOTS and STRESS into Level 2; Virtual Recruiter reaches level 3. MRES and deLearyous did not provide enough information to be classified into one of the levels. The fact that only one of the projects went beyond level 2 can probably be explained by the difficulty to measure the real impact of training intervention, as well as the costs (in terms of time and money) involved in it. Also, as most of the applications were the result of academic endeavours from computer scientists, more extensive evaluation efforts were probably not high on their priority list. Nevertheless, to make IVAs for social skills training more widely adopted, it would be wise to spend more time on longitudinal studies with the aim to assess how effective these systems are in changing a person's behaviour.

4.6 Formalism

The column on formalisms has been included to provide an overview of the programming languages, modelling frameworks, and other tools that have been used to implement the IVA-based systems that were reviewed. As can be seen, the technology used varies from standard programming language (such as C#) and general AI tools (such as AIML) to more dedicated agent-based development frameworks (such as InterACT or PsychSim). Clearly, as each project uses its own approach, it is hard to draw any useful conclusion from this information. Perhaps the most important lesson that can be learned from this is that it is advisable to strive towards a more uniform standard for the development of IVAs (e.g., the Virtual Human Toolkit [5]).

5 Conclusion

This paper discussed twelve different applications which all share the aim to improve a user's social skills. The focus was on social skills training in the professional domain. Although there was a wide variety in the approaches taken to reach this goal, there are also some similarities between different applications. An overview of the differences and similarities can be found in Tables 1 and 2. However, it is important to note that not all papers provided the same amount of background information.

It is impossible to conclude that there is one single approach that works best in all situations. Rather, the choice for a certain paradigm or technology should depend on the purpose of the training application. As a general approach, when developing an IVA-based training system, it is useful to view the envisioned system in terms of the architecture displayed in Fig. 1. Then, for each module in the architecture, an entire spectrum of methods is available (e.g., for the 'input part' one can distinguish between free speech, free text, multiple choice, etc). The developer should select the method that is most suitable for the intended purpose, considering the relevant financial, temporal and other constraints. In addition, more effort should be spent on long-term studies that assess how effective IVA-based systems really are in changing a person's behaviour, and which factors contribute to that.

Acknowledgements. This research was supported by the Brazilian scholarship program Science without Borders - CNPq scholarship reference: 233883/2014-2.

References

1. Bates, J., et al.: The role of emotion in believable agents. Commun. ACM **37**(7), 122–125 (1994)
2. Beskow, J., Peters, C., Castellano, G., O'Sullivan, C., Leite, I., Kopp, S.: Intelligent Virtual Agents. LNCS. Springer, Cham (2017). https://doi.org/10.1007/978-3-319-67401-8

3. Bosch, K., Bosse, T., de Jong, S.: Trainen met gesimuleerde mensen: Effectief inzetten van gedragsmodellen voor militaire training. Militaire Spectator **9**(184), 358–373 (2015)
4. Hargie, O.: Handbook of Communication Skills. Routledge, Abingdon (1997)
5. Hartholt, A., et al.: All together now. In: Aylett, R., Krenn, B., Pelachaud, C., Shimodaira, H. (eds.) IVA 2013. LNCS (LNAI), vol. 8108, pp. 368–381. Springer, Heidelberg (2013). https://doi.org/10.1007/978-3-642-40415-3_33
6. Heuvelink, A., Mioch, T.: FeGA: a feedback generating agent. In: Proceedings of the Seventh IEEE/WIC/ACM International Conference on Intelligent Agent Technology, IAT 2008, pp. 567–572 (2008)
7. Jense, G., Kuijper, F.: Virtual environments for advanced trainers and simulators. Z. pl.: Z. uitg. (1993)
8. Kirkpatrick, J.D., Kirkpatrick, W.K.: Kirkpatrick's Four Levels of Training Evaluation. Association for Talent Development, Alexandria (2016)
9. Leuski, A., Traum, D.: NPCEditor: creating virtual human dialogue using information retrieval techniques. AI Mag. **32**(2), 42–56 (2011)
10. Maguire, P., Pitceathly, C.: Key communication skills and how to acquire them. BMJ **325**(7366), 697–700 (2002)
11. Provoost, S., Lau, H.M., Ruwaard, J., Riper, H.: Embodied conversational agents in clinical psychology: a scoping review. J. Med. Internet Res. **19**(5), e51 (2017)
12. Slater, M.: Place illusion and plausibility can lead to realistic behaviour in immersive virtual environments. Phil. Trans. Roy. Soc. B: Biol. Sci. **364**(1535), 3549–3557 (2009)
13. Slovak, P., Thieme, A., Murphy, D., Tennent, P., Olivier, P., Fitzgerald, G.: On becoming a counsellor: challenges and opportunities to support interpersonal skills development. In: Proceedings of the 18th ACM Conference on Computer Supported Cooperative Work and Social Computing, CSCW 2015, pp. 1336–1347 (2015)
14. Stokoe, E.: Simulated interaction and communication skills training: the 'Conversation-Analytic Role-Play Method'. In: Antaki, C. (ed.) Applied Conversation Analysis, Palgrave Advances in Linguistics. Palgrave Macmillan, London (2011). https://doi.org/10.1057/9780230316874_7
15. Todorov, E., Shadmehr, R., Bizzi, E.: Augmented feedback presented in a virtual environment accelerates learning of a difficult motor task. J. Motor Behav. **29**(2), 147–158 (1997)
16. Van Raaij, E.M., Schepers, J.J.: The acceptance and use of a virtual learning environment in China. Comput. Educ. **50**(3), 838–852 (2008)
17. Wang, S., O'Brien-Pallas, L.L., Hayes, L.: A Review and Evaluation of Workplace Violence Prevention Programs in the Health Sector. Nursing Health Services Research Unit, Toronto (2008)
18. Wolf, T.: Assessing student learning in a virtual laboratory environment. IEEE Trans. Educ. **53**(2), 216–222 (2010)
19. Zyda, M.: From visual simulation to virtual reality to games. Computer **38**(9), 25–32 (2005)

A Machine Learning Approach to Detect Violent Behaviour from Video

David Nova[1], André Ferreira[2], and Paulo Cortez[1]($\boxtimes$) (iD)

[1] ALGORITMI Centre, Department of Information Systems, University of Minho,
4804-533 Guimarães, Portugal
pcortez@dsi.uminho.pt

[2] Department of Informatics, University of Minho, 4710-057 Braga, Portugal

Abstract. The automatic classification of violent actions performed by two or more persons is an important task for both societal and scientific purposes. In this paper, we propose a machine learning approach, based a Support Vector Machine (SVM), to detect if a human action, captured on a video, is or not violent. Using a pose estimation algorithm, we focus mostly on feature engineering, to generate the SVM inputs. In particular, we hand-engineered a set of input features based on keypoints (angles, velocity and contact detection) and used them, under distinct combinations, to study their effect on violent behavior recognition from video. Overall, an excellent classification was achieved by the best performing SVM model, which used keypoints, angles and contact features computed over a 60 frame image input range.

Keywords: Machine learning · Support Vector Machine ·
Action recognition · Pose estimation · Video analysis

1 Introduction

Nowadays, human behaviour is increasingly being recorded using digital cameras [1,13,24]. Following this increase of video data, there is a growing need for the development of intelligent video analysis systems, capable of providing value in several real-world domains, including video surveillance, human-robot interactions, entertainment and health applications, marketing and retail management [2,14]. In this work, we focus on violent action detection, which is potentially useful in several real-world scenarios, such as to assist security personnel or to perform emergency calls.

Pose estimation or skeleton detection is a key tool for human action analysis from video [2,10,17]. In this paper, we use a pose estimation algorithm, running on the background of a video, to extract the key points of all human subjects. From the collected keypoint coordinates, we derive three new distinct features (angles, velocity and contact detection), which are then merged with the keypoint coordinates, leading to an input feature vector. The generated dataset is used to

© ICST Institute for Computer Sciences, Social Informatics and Telecommunications Engineering 2019
Published by Springer Nature Switzerland AG 2019. All Rights Reserved
P. Cortez et al. (Eds.): INTETAIN 2018, LNICST 273, pp. 85–94, 2019.
https://doi.org/10.1007/978-3-030-16447-8_9

train a Support Vector Machine (SVM), which predicts if there is a violent action. The set of features includes the velocity of all keypoints, six differently disposed angles and whether the persons are in contact or not. The extraction of features was done using a temporal frame step, which was set at 60 or 120 frames. A total of 32 different configuration experimental tests were performed. Overall, an excellent classification performance was achieved by the best performing model.

The paper is organized as follows. Section 2 presents the related work. Next, Sect. 3 describes the video data, machine learning approach and evaluation. Then, Sect. 4 details the experiments held and analyses the obtained results. Finally, Sect. 5 discusses the main conclusions.

2   Related Work

Due to the recent advances in deep learning algorithms, the use of convolutional neural networks (CNN) to predict actions on videos or images has seen a considerable growth. These methods are often paired with skeletons or other local features extracted from pose estimation algorithms, such as motion [4], to better model the action performed. Another deep learning approach was proposed in [26], which used a 3D CNN integrated with a Markov chain model to infer pose and motion from video frames. More recently, CNNs were used in [18] to extract visual information derived from temporal progression of joint coordinates.

For video object detection and classification, several other neural networks have been proposed. The ResNet architecture uses RGB images with encoded spatial-temporal features extracted from 3D skeleton keypoints [11,20]. In 2018, the ResNet model was extended, under five distinct architectures, in [21]. Other new neural networks, handcrafted for the detection of actions, have also been proposed, such as the Attentional Recurrent Relational Network - Long Short Term Memory (ARNN-LSTM)[16].

Regarding the task of violent action detection, which is a subset of the general human action recognition, it has been mainly addressed by using handcrafted input features, which often concentrate on visual cues found in images. For instance, in 1997, Vasconcelos and Lippman [23] used the the bodies in different frames to calculate the variation undergone throughout the video. In 2006, this method was improved by detecting blood regions on skin and analyzing them for motion intensity [5]. In 2002, motion trajectory and the orientation of different body limbs present on a frame was used to detect violent acts from video [7]. In 2014, the acceleration of body parts, as derived from the variation of the bodies on subsequent frames, was adopted in [8]. More recently, in 2016, LSTM deep learning networks were used to solve the problem of missing temporal information, on which visual features (extracted using CNN), optical flow images and acceleration flow maps were followed by an LSTM and were subject to a late fusion [9]. Expanding on this work, in 2017 the AlexNet architecture [15] was adopted [22]. The model used as inputs two subsequent frames at each step, as a mean to encode a visual representation vector that was sent to a convolutional LSTM network. After processing the frames, several fully connected layers compute the final classification.

In this paper, we work with new visual hand-crafted features, such as angles, velocity and contact between two human subjects. These features are merged in order to encode temporal information and create a feature vector that is fed to a binary classification SVM model, aiming to predict violent behaviour.

3   Materials and Methods

3.1   Video Data

In this work, we adopted the ISR-UoL 3D Social Activity Dataset [6], which contains a total of 93660 RGB images of multi-person actions, divided into 10 sessions. Each session contains 8 different acts and it is composed of a unique combination of two persons. A person can appear in another sessions, but not paired up in a similar combination. Every act represents a unique action repeated throughout the 10 different sessions. The specific personal nuances that each person exhibits when performing actions are herein captured and help increase the generalization of the dataset. An act can sometimes be divided into 4 mini-recordings, each with the same act. The dataset contains the skeleton data, the RGB data and the depth data for each image. There are a total of 8 distinct human actions:

1. handshake - 17460 video frames;
2. hug - 15084 frames;
3. help walk - 9592 frames;
4. help stand-up - 3123 frames;
5. **fight** - 16465 frames;
6. **push** - 18739 frames;
7. talk - 17895 frames; and
8. draw attention - 15920 frames.

The human actions were performed by a group of 6 people, from which 4 are male and 2 are female. For the binary target output class, we assumed the push and fight as violent or aggressive actions (around 31% of the frames), while the other classes are considered as non-violent. We note that the violent actions (fight and push) were clearly staged, in order to avoid physical injuries.

   The images were derived from a set of small videos, with a duration of around 40 to 60 s, recorded at a frame rate of 30 frames per second. The videos capture the entire body of the subjects involved on an action, which allows for a total pose estimation inference. Figure 1 presents a few examples of the human actions present in the dataset.

3.2   Machine Learning Approach

The adopted pose estimation algorithm was OpenPose [3]. This algorithm was developed and it is currently supported by the CMU Perceptual Computing Lab. It uses Part Affinity Fields (PAFs) to learn how to connect the limbs of an

Fig. 1. Examples of human actions from the dataset: draw attention (top left); hug (top right); handshake (bottom left); and fight (bottom right)

individual and heatmaps to successfully identify multiple people in an image. It was developed using the programming language C++ and the machine learning library `Caffe`. Initially, the model was trained using the template used on the COCO keypoints dataset, with 18 different joints that when connected form a pose. More recently, a model with a total of 25 joints was released. This model considers all the previous points plus a higher concentration/detail on the foot. In this paper, we either retrieve the full 25 points or the first 9 points, which correspond to the human torso area.

Physical contact between two people, be it abrupt and quick or soft and slow, should be a strong indicator for identifying violent behaviour. In our work, it corresponds to the first extracted feature. After laying out the structure of the tree-shaped body and how the keypoints are placed on the model, we initially used box shape to envelope the body of a person. However, in preliminary experiments, we found that the box tend to include a large portion of the background of the image. Thus, wrap the human body with a more natural human-polygon based shape, aiming to detect a contact while reducing the background clutter to a minimum. We automatically detect a contact when two human-polygons have an intersection area.

With the periodic information provided by OpenPose, it is possible to calculate the velocity of one or all the limbs of a person. The velocity feature can be used to detect which limbs are moving quicker and more often than others. The feature is calculated comparing and then subtracting the positions of the current keypoints with the positions of the previous ones, then dividing by the time between two consecutive image frames. It should be noted that we use zero velocity values in case of the first frame of a video action scene. The velocity, in our experiments, is estimated for all the keypoints of a skeleton. For example, if 9 keypoints are used then we compute 9 velocity values.

Human anatomy restricts each joint to a specific range of angles, in which movement is allowed without any direct damage to the body integrity. As such, the angles on which certain joints are encountered on specific actions may be a clear indicator for the detection of such action. The angles were calculated using the following formula:

$$Angle = \frac{(\arctan(AB_y, AB_x) - \arctan(CB_x, CB_y)) \times 180}{\pi} \tag{1}$$

where AB_y and AB_x represent the distance, on the y and x axis, from point A to point B. Similarly, CB_x and CB_y represent the distances between points C and B. We extract 6 different angles when all 25 keypoints are used, which are localized on the right and left, elbows, shoulders and knees. When the keypoints are reduced to 9, only 4 angles are computed (by removing the right and left knees).

OpenPose cannot distinguish between two different persons. In practice, this means that the keypoints outputted by the pose algorithm can differ in order and in an irregular and unreliable way. To solve this issue, we developed a tracking algorithm, described as follows. At the beginning of the algorithm, the tracking algorithm Kernelized Correlation Filters (KCF) [12] is initialized and the Region of Interest (ROI) is established overlapping the throat joint, saving into an array the order and the keypoints from every person detected on the first frame. Then, a conditional rule checks whether the actual frame is the second frame or not. If it is, the algorithm resets the tracker defining its ROI as the throat joint and then resets the counter. If it is not, it adds 1 to the counter and updates the tracker. After that, the algorithm draws the updated tracker boxes and changes the array created at the beginning, with the new keypoints, if the actual keypoints of the point 1 are inside the updated tracker box. Figure 2 exemplifies the distinct extracted features.

The extracted image features were stored in CSV files (one per each video scene), with each column corresponding to a different feature and each row to a different frame. Typically, each video action has a duration of four minutes. To achieve shorted classification results, we designed the SVM classifier to work with very short video sequences, with a length up to 2 (60 frames) or 4 s (120 frames). We achieve this, the CSV files were preprocessed in order to create a short video sequence input feature vector, which is fed the SVM. Thus, the feature vector contains the concatenation of all considered features (NF) for all short sequence images (SS) of the scene ($SS = 60$ or $SS = 120$ frames). Thus, the input feature vector length is $NF \times SI$.

As for the learning model, we used a fast SVM variant, capable of working with high dimensional input features, and that used a linear kernel.

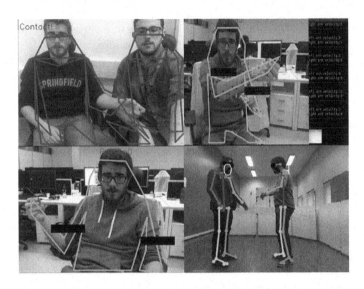

Fig. 2. Examples of the features extracted: contact detection (top left); velocity (top right); angles (bottom left); and tracking (bottom right)

3.3 Evaluation

A confusion matrix allows to visualize the results obtained by a classification algorithm. Each row of the matrix corresponds to an instance of a predicted class while the columns represent the actual (desired) classes. For a given class c, the matrix exhibits the values of true positives (TP_c), false positives (FP_c), false negatives (FNc) and true negatives (TNc). Using this matrix, several performance metrics can be computed, such as Precision, Recall and F1-Score [25]:

$$Precision = \frac{TP_c}{TP_c + FP_c} \tag{2}$$

$$Recall = \frac{TP_c}{TP_c + FN_c} \tag{3}$$

$$F1\text{-}Score = 2\frac{Precision_c * Recall_c}{Precision_c + Recall_c} \tag{4}$$

To aggregate the violent and non-violent class metrics into a single measure, we adopted the weight-averaging method, which weights the measure according to the class prevalence in the data.

To validate the predictive models, we used the standard holdout train/test validation split [19]. The split was based on the dataset sessions: data from by data from sessions 1 to 7 were included in the training set (70%) and images from sessions 8 to 10 were used in the to test set (30%).

4   Results

4.1   Computational Environment

The experiments were conducted using code written in the Python language. In particular, we adopted the Python API available at the OpenPose library [3] to interact with the pose algorithm. Since the experiments required a substantial computational effort, we conducted them using a dedicated machine with an Intel i7-7800X processor and a GeForce GTX 1080 Ti.

Several components of the designed computational experimentation were implemented using known Python modules, namely: Shapely – to detect the intersection of two distinct polygons; csv – to write the extract features into the CSV format; Numpy – to handle the feature vector, concatenating the features from different frames; and scikit-learn – to run the SVM algorithm and compute the classification performance metrics. We also adopted the OpenCV tracking API to load the images from the dataset and implement the KCF tracking algorithm. As for the SVM implementation, we used the L2 penalty, a soft margin parameter of $C = 1$, and a training that performs a maximum of 1000 iterations.

4.2   Violent Action Detection Results

The number of executed experiments was $E = D \times F = 4 \times 8 = 32$ experiments, with $D = 4$ dataset combinations and $F = 8$ feature setups. The datasets include 25 or 9 keypoints, with a lenght of 60 or 120 frames: A – 25 keypoints and 120 frames; B – 25 keypoints and 60 frames; C – 9 keypoints and 60 frames; and D – 9 keypoints and 120 frames. As for the features, we explored the following setups: 1 – keypoints only; 2 – keypoints and angles; 3 – keypoints and velocities; 4 – keypoints and contact; 5 – keypoints, angles and velocities; 6 – keypoints, angles and contact; 7 – keypoints, contact and velocities; and 8 – all features. Table 1 presents the overall F1-score values for each tested configuration. In the table, each configuration (column **Model**) is represented by the respective combination letter and feature digit. Overall, the best result was obtained for the configuration that uses 60 frames and a set of input features composed of 25 keypoints, 6 angles and 1 contact (A6). For this selected model, detailed classification results are presented in Table 2 and Fig. 3. The total number of features used by the model is $NF = (25 \times 2 \ (x \text{ and } y \text{ axis}) \times 2 \ (\text{two people})) + (6 \times 2 \ (\text{people})) + 1 = 113$. As shown in Fig. 3, the proposed SVM presents high true positive (85%) and true negative (92%) rates. Globally, high quality Precision, Recall and F1-score classification measures were achieved (89%, Table 2).

Table 1. Classification results for all experiments (best value in **bold**)

Model	F1-score	Model	F1-score	Model	F1-score	Model	F1-score
A1	0.87	A3	0.88	A5	0.88	A7	0.88
B1	0.87	B3	0.84	B5	0.85	B7	0.85
C1	0.87	C3	0.87	C5	0.81	C7	0.88
D1	0.84	D3	0.83	D5	0.83	D7	0.85
A2	0.88	A4	0.87	**A6**	**0.89**	A8	0.88
B2	0.84	B4	0.86	B6	0.85	B8	0.84
C2	0.84	C4	0.86	C6	0.82	C8	0.79
D2	0.84	D4	0.86	D6	0.83	D8	0.81

Table 2. Classification measures for the selected A6 model

Number of features (NF)	Precision	Recall	F1-score
113	0.89	0.89	0.89

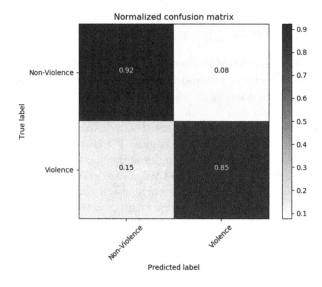

Fig. 3. Normalized confusion matrix for the selected A6 model

5   Conclusions

Currently, there is a vast amount of human daily activities that are recorded using digital cameras. Thus, automated systems capable of detecting interesting human behaviour from video are valuable in several real-world scenarios.

In this paper, we target violent action detection by using short video sequences (60 or 120 frames) and hand-engineered features: skeleton keypoints;

angles and velocities computed over these keypoints; and contact detection based on human-polygon shapes. As the base learning classifier, we adopted the popular Support Vector Machine (SVM), with a linear kernel. A large set of 32 experiments was executed, by considering different short input video sequences (60 or 120 frames), number of keypoints (25 or 9), and velocity, angles and contact combinations. The system was tested on the publicly available ISR-UoL 3D Social Activity dataset, with a total of 93660 images reflecting 8 human actions. We have merged the 8 distinct actions into violent (fight and push) and non-violent examples (other actions). The best performing model used a short video sequence of 60 frames (1 s), 25 skeleton keypoints, 6 angels and human contact detection. Overall, an excellent classification performance was achieved, with a Precision, Recall and F1-score values of 89%.

In the future, we intend to extend this work by enriching the set of features (e.g., acceleration values, 3D skeleton data). We also plan to perform experiments that consider distinct video scenarios (e.g, with more than two people, inside a closer space such as a vehicle).

Acknowledgments. The work of P. Cortez was supported by Fundação para a Ciência e Tecnologia (FCT) within the Project Scope: UID/CEC/00319/2013.

References

1. Afsar, P., Cortez, P., Santos, H.: Automatic visual detection of human behavior: a review from 2000 to 2014. Expert Syst. Appl. **42**(20), 6935–6956 (2015). https://doi.org/10.1016/j.eswa.2015.05.023
2. Afsar, P., Cortez, P., Santos, H.M.D.: Automatic human trajectory destination prediction from video. Expert Syst. Appl. **110**, 41–51 (2018). https://doi.org/10.1016/j.eswa.2018.03.035
3. Cao, Z., Simon, T., Wei, S.E., Sheikh, Y.: Realtime multi-person 2D pose estimation using part affinity fields. In: CVPR (2017)
4. Chéron, G., Laptev, I., Schmid, C.: P-CNN: pose-based CNN features for action recognition. CoRR abs/1506.03607 (2015). http://arxiv.org/abs/1506.03607
5. Clarin, C.T., Dionisio, J.A.M., Echavez, M.T., Naval, P.C.: DOVE: detection of movie violence using motion intensity analysis on skin and blood. Technical report, University of the Philippines (2005)
6. Coppola, C., Faria, D., Nunes, U., Bellotto, N.: Social activity recognition based on probabilistic merging of skeleton features with proximity priors from RGB-D data. In: Proceedings of IEEE/RSJ International Conference on Intelligent Robots and Systems (IROS), pp. 5055–5061 (2016)
7. Datta, A., Shah, M., Lobo, N.D.V.: Person-on-person violence detection in video data. In: Object Recognition Supported by User Interaction for Service Robots, vol. 1, pp. 433–438, August 2002. https://doi.org/10.1109/ICPR.2002.1044748
8. Deniz, O., Serrano, I., Bueno, G., Kim, T.: Fast violence detection in video. In: 2014 International Conference on Computer Vision Theory and Applications (VISAPP), vol. 2, pp. 478–485, January 2014
9. Dong, Z., Qin, J., Wang, Y.: Multi-stream deep networks for person to person violence detection in videos. In: Tan, T., Li, X., Chen, X., Zhou, J., Yang, J., Cheng, H. (eds.) Pattern Recognition, pp. 517–531. Springer, Singapore (2016). https://doi.org/10.1007/978-981-10-3002-4_43

10. Du, W., Wang, Y., Qiao, Y.: RPAN: an end-to-end recurrent pose-attention net-work for action recognition in videos. In: 2017 IEEE International Conference on Computer Vision (ICCV), pp. 3745–3754, October 2017. https://doi.org/10.1109/ICCV.2017.402
11. He, K., Zhang, X., Ren, S., Sun, J.: Deep residual learning for image recognition. CoRR abs/1512.03385 (2015). http://arxiv.org/abs/1512.03385
12. Henriques, J.F., Caseiro, R., Martins, P., Batista, J.: High-speed tracking with kernelized correlation filters. CoRR abs/1404.7584 (2014). http://arxiv.org/abs/1404.7584
13. Herath, S., Harandi, M.T., Porikli, F.: Going deeper into action recognition: a survey. CoRR abs/1605.04988 (2016). http://arxiv.org/abs/1605.04988
14. Kong, Y., Fu, Y.: Human Action Recognition and Prediction: A Survey. ArXiv e-prints, June 2018
15. Krizhevsky, A., Sutskever, I., Hinton, G.E.: ImageNet classification with deep con-volutional neural networks. In: Pereira, F., Burges, C.J.C., Bottou, L., Weinberger, K.Q. (eds.) Advances in Neural Information Processing Systems, vol. 25, pp. 1097–1105. Curran Associates, Inc. (2012). http://papers.nips.cc/paper/4824-imagenet-classification-with-deep-convolutional-neural-networks.pdf
16. Li, L., Zheng, W., Zhang, Z., Huang, Y., Wang, L.: Skeleton-based relational mod-eling for action recognition. CoRR abs/1805.02556 (2018). http://arxiv.org/abs/1805.02556
17. Liu, J., Shahroudy, A., Xu, D., Wang, G.: Spatio-temporal LSTM with trust gates for 3D human action recognition. CoRR abs/1607.07043 (2016). http://arxiv.org/abs/1607.07043
18. Luvizon, D.C., Picard, D., Tabia, H.: 2D/3D pose estimation and action recognition using multitask deep learning. CoRR abs/1802.09232 (2018). http://arxiv.org/abs/1802.09232
19. Ng, A.: Machine Learning Yearning. deeplearning.ai (2018)
20. Pham, H., Khoudour, L., Crouzil, A., Zegers, P., Velastin, S.A.: Exploiting deep residual networks for human action recognition from skeletal data. CoRR abs/1803.07781 (2018). http://arxiv.org/abs/1803.07781
21. Pham, H., Khoudour, L., Crouzil, A., Zegers, P., Velastin, S.A.: Learning and recog-nizing human action from skeleton movement with deep residual neural networks. CoRR abs/1803.07780 (2018). http://arxiv.org/abs/1803.07780
22. Sudhakaran, S., Lanz, O.: Learning to detect violent videos using convolutional long short-term memory. CoRR abs/1709.06531 (2017). http://arxiv.org/abs/1709.06531
23. Vasconcelos, N., Lippman, A.: Towards semantically meaningful feature spaces for the characterization of video content. In: Proceedings of International Conference on Image Processing, vol. 1, pp. 25–28, October 1997. https://doi.org/10.1109/ICIP.1997.647375
24. Wang, Q.: A survey of visual analysis of human motion and its applications. CoRR abs/1608.00700 (2016). http://arxiv.org/abs/1608.00700
25. Witten, I., Frank, E., Hall, M., Pal, C.: Data Mining: Practical Machine Learning Tools and Techniques, 4th edn. Morgan Kaufmann, San Franscico (2017)
26. Zolfaghari, M., Oliveira, G.L., Sedaghat, N., Brox, T.: Chained multi-stream net-works exploiting pose, motion, and appearance for action classification and detec-tion. CoRR abs/1704.00616 (2017). http://arxiv.org/abs/1704.00616

Detection and Prevention of Bullying on Online Social Networks: The Combination of Textual, Visual and Cognitive

Carlos Silva$^{(\boxtimes)}$, Ricardo Santos⬥, and Ricardo Barbosa⬥

CIICESI - Center for Research and Innovation in Business Sciences
and Information Systems, School of Management and Technology,
Polytechnic Institute of Porto, Felgueiras, Portugal
{8120333,rjs,rmb}@estg.ipp.pt

Abstract. The adoption of online social platforms as a common space for the virtualisation of identities is also correlated with the replication of real-world social hazards in the virtual world. Bullying, or cyberbullying, is a very common practice among people nowadays, becoming much more present due to the increase of online time, especially in online social networks, and having more serious consequences among younger audiences. Related work includes the analysis and classification of textual characteristics that can be indicative of a bullying situation and even a visual analysis approach through the adoption of image recognition techniques. While agreeing that the combination of textual and visual analysis can help the identification of bullying practice, or the identification of bullies, we also believe that a part is missing. In this work, we propose a combination of textual and visual classification techniques, associated with a cognitive aspect that can help to identify possible bullies. Based on a previous model definition for a virtual social sensor, we propose the analysis of textual content present on online social networks, check the presence of people in multimedia content, and identification of the stakeholders on a possible bullying situation by identifying cognitive characteristics and similarities on the behaviours of possible bullies and/or victims. This identification of possible bullying scenario can help to address them before they occur or reach unmanageable proportions.

Keywords: Online social networks · Bullying · Virtual social sensor · Cognitive

1 Introduction

The high dependence on the computer and mobile devices, whether to professional or academic work, either for leisure or other activities such as reading news or consulting social networks, is strongly present on the Internet. The Internet is a great asset because it allows us to be connected to any part of the world in a fraction of a second, enabling us to access any information in real time, and it can override other methods that would take us much longer to achieve certain goals. However, it is not full of wonders, and

P. Cortez et al. (Eds.): INTETAIN 2018, LNICST 273, pp. 95–104, 2019.
https://doi.org/10.1007/978-3-030-16447-8_10

each user is constantly susceptible to the range of some attacks such as virus or phishing and is subject to believe in misleading information.

Children spend some time with the new technologies and accessing the Internet in an uncontrolled way by their parents or tutors may lead them to use it improperly. The visualization of content that they should not have access to, could make them a target for social hazards. Focusing on the usage of online social networks (Facebook, Twitter, Youtube, Instagram, just to name a few) we face a set of problems like lack of privacy, or even the possibility of being victims of insult or other harming situations, in order words, bullying.

Bullying is a complex social dynamic, motivated essentially by differences of the domain, social capital or culture [1]. The desire for dominance, acquisition and maintenance of social capital are the main factors of motivation for the initiation and prolongation of the practice of bullying. For example, the lack of social capital by the victims may impede them from getting a better social position or the capacity to acquiring a specific thing, which may lead to contempt from the others. In addition, the denomination used by aggressors, also known as bullies, to subjugate the victims, results in an intense humiliation that has negative effects on such people, like anger and depression.

Cyberbullying, like traditional bullying, has a profound negative impact on the victim, especially when dealing with children and young people, suffering significantly in one emotional and psychological way, even with some cases ending in tragic suicides. So, cyberbullying can be described as: when the Internet, mobile phones or other devices are used to send text or images that can hurt, humiliate or embarrass other people, and it is a more constant version of the traditional bullying [2].

Unlike spam, this kind of attack is more personal, varied and contextual [3]. The images published by an individual in a social network, the type of content shared, the links comments and the possibility of easy exchange of messages with any other user, allow the practice of bullying to be more frequent and constant than ever, and it is a danger that must be considered in our society.

In this work, we aim to address this problem by combining three main types of classification techniques: textual; visual; and cognitive. Taking as base a previously defined virtual social sensor model, we enhance its capabilities by providing new modules that can help the identification of bullying situations, correctly identification of bullies, and the possibility to identify potential bullies, or bullying situations, through the analysis of personality traits (that are directly responsible for our behaviour).

This work is divided as follows: Sect. 2 describes the main problems that arise on the Internet, and introduces the topic of online bullying, or cyberbullying; Sect. 3 is dedicated to an overview look of the work already developed in this subject, describing the approaches and technologies used for the development and implementation. In Sect. 4 we describe our solution proposal, which includes the combination of the three main characteristics (textual, visual, and cognitive) as an approach to correctly identify bullies, bullying, and other social hazards. This work ends with a conclusion and definition of the future work.

2   Internet as a Threat

Our constant need to be connected with the world, either for short periodic interactions, or for prolonged activities like viewing the news, email, interact in social platforms, or talk with a customer or partner in order to conduct deals, makes unbelievable to live without the Internet. The Internet allows us to perform an infinite number of tasks and is intended to simplify the life of those who use it, becoming an added value for society. However, behind all those benefits, its usage hides a negative side.

A study [4] analysed children behaviour on the Internet across several countries, and from all risks present across the web for children, (between 11 and 16 years old) the authors identified that 5% of the respondents (about 3500 in total) already suffered bullying, and another 5% received messages of a sexual nature, however, only 3% felt bothered by that situation. Meeting new people was reported by 11% of the children, and none of them felt uncomfortable with that. The contact with images that contained nudity or pornographic content was experienced by 27%, and other types of content related to hate, self-harming, anorexia and drugs were reached by 10%. The contact with the technologies and the Internet begins by playing games, which in many cases require connection to the Internet, and may allow connection to other unknown players in any part of the planet. Then, they need to use the web for research to the accomplishment of school works, followed by joining social networks, mainly Facebook, Twitter and Instagram. This data shows that children begin to have access to technology in a prematurely way, coinciding mostly with the period in which they are attending the first cycle of basic education.

Recently, big organisations like Google or Facebook, are taking more attention to these situations to implement web-based security programs, against several types of hazards. This kind of actions would be necessary to help avoid facing these situations, despite the existence of advisor programs that alert people for some of these cases that are broadcasted mainly in the schools and in the traditional media (like television or newspaper). The introduction of automatic mechanisms may prevent the occurrence of some of these problems or control them to avoid scaling up without control.

2.1   Bullying Is also Cyberbullying

On the Internet, it is common to have a reflection of some social problems that exist in the real world, like bullying. Bullying is the process of threatening or assaulting an individual or a group of individuals towards others, usually related to some characteristic of their lives, as their culture, and is more common among young people.

On the virtual world, the practice of bullying, or cyberbullying, is performed by repeated psychological violence acts, practised by one youth or groups of young people over another, using technologies, either using Internet applications or directly through text messages and telephone calls. Unlike traditional bullying, bullying through technologies do not lead to physical contact, unless those involved met on daily bases, such as at school, where the situation can get worse. However, given that young people spend a lot of time with their technological devices, especially for checking and updating of their social networks, this practice of violence becomes more constant, harder to identify, and more conducive to humiliation with a higher number of people reached.

McClowry et al. [5] divide bullying into two types: direct, entails blatant attacks on a targeted young person; indirect, involves communication with others about the targeted individual (spreading harmful rumours). The authors also refer out that bullying can be physical, verbal or relational (excluding someone, denying friendship) and may involve property damage. Boys tend to do more direct bullying behaviours, while girls are more involved in acts related to indirect bullying.

Hee et al. [6] describe three main roles in a bullying scenario, the bully, the victim and bystanders. The bullies are those ones who intend to attack or threat someone, the victims correspond to the people who suffer bullying from others and bystanders are those who also view the post and sometimes interact in it. They can show up to support the victim and mitigate the negative effects caused by the bullying or can be an active part in the bullying, joining the attacker and making the situation go worse or can simply ignore the evidence and keep scrolling on the news feed.

But why would anyone take the initiative to attack another? In many cases, the bully has been a victim before, making him a more furious and aggressive person causing him to use that anger on someone, feels solitude and needs attention, has problems at home, or has low self-esteem and to feel better tries to degrade others. The bully may also want to have more popularity and attacks people he feels jealous of, can have a big ego, may feel superior to others, and has a security group in most of the cases to feel safe if someone riposte to his attacks [7]. Often, these attacks are linked to sensitive topics such as race and culture, sexuality, intelligence, physical appearance, and aspects that people cannot change about themselves [2].

Sometimes the target of offensive messages on the Internet is also the one who writes them, sending it to themselves, under a pseudonym. The motives for that vary, from young people who do it as a form of fun, to people who want to test the reaction of some friends, or cases of depressed individuals who want to make themselves feel even worse. This behaviour is more prevalent in adolescents who do not identify themselves as heterosexuals and in people who had been victims of bullying in the past. Boys are also more likely to send offensive messages to themselves, usually as a joke to get the attention of friends, or love interests [8].

Cyberbullying is also much more likely to be done by someone the victim knows well. Children are seven times more likely to be attacked by current or former friends or romantic interests than by any stranger. More than a third of adults harassed on the web do not know the person who is harassing them, and just less than a third are harassed by people who hide their identities. Homosexual students are more likely to be victims of these acts, as are non-white students. Girls are 2.6 times more likely to be victims than boys, and woman are 2 times more likely to be harassed online. In some cases, through fake accounts, the attacker tries to impersonate the victim, publishing content to humiliate that person [9]. Bullies normally post less, participate in fewer online communities, and are less popular than normal users [10].

This kind of attack may look easy to dismiss, however, the perpetrator blackmails the victim with the threat of publication of content that he has received before, such as private information or intimate photos, and some physical threats to the victim family can lead to a more serious situation than it seemed initially. Assuming that being online is increasingly necessary whether for employment tasks or academic works, is simply not possible to turn off your computer to stop receiving these attacks.

Some studies present a distinction between cyberbullying and cyberaggression. Cyberaggression is defined as aggressive online behaviour that uses digital media in a way that is intended to cause harm to another person. Cyberbullying is one form of cyberaggression that is more restrictively defined as an act of aggression online with an imbalance of power between the individuals involved and repetition of the aggression [11].

3 Related Work

Cyberbullying is a serious social problem especially among adolescents, and it is defined as the use of technology to deliberately or repeatedly attack others. With the emergence of online social networks, this phenomenon has become more prevalent.

Huang et al. [12] used a Twitter corpus to identify social and textual features to create a composite model to automatically detect cyberbullying. They built graphs related to the social network and derived a set of features, to see the context of "me", "my friends" and the relationship between them, setting weights to the edges to represent interactions between users. The authors indicate that victims of cyberbullying may have a significantly lower self-esteem compared to others and are likely to be more active in networks. They also take a look at the popularity and activity of the users and the number of publications between them. This approach implied the verification of the density of bad words ("asshole", "bitch") and hieroglyphs ("5hit", "@ss"), capital letters rate, the number of exclamation and questions marks, the number of emojis, also checking the part-of-speech (POS) tags and trying to detect text like "you are" or "yourself".

The study *Modeling the Detection of Textual Cyberbullying* [2] focuses on analysing a corpus of comments from Youtube videos linked to sensitive topics such as race and culture, sexuality, intelligence, or physical appearance. They removed stop words, the non-important sequence of characters (for example, the last character repetitions in "lollll"), and the links for users (e.g., @username). For text classification, they do two experiments: training binary classifiers to check if an instance can be classified for more than one sensible topic; using multi-class classifiers to classify an instance of a set of sensitive topics. They concluded that binary classifiers work best on this problem. The tools used were the Naïve Bayes and Support Vector Machines as classifiers, J48 and JRip as learning methods. In the end, they report that the most difficult sentences to detect are those that contain sarcasm or irony because they do not usually contain the negative words that we are looking for to identify the problem.

Chatzakou et al. [10] characterize a Twitter user by its publications across the time. They classify a user in one of this four categories: aggressive, bullying, spammer or normal. They emphasise the importance to collect some of his profile information like the account age, number of followers and tweet history, especially to check if his kind of speech is constant or if it changed across the time.

Zhao et al. [13] present a mechanism for automatic detection of cyberbullying in social networks through a set of defined bullying features. First, they define a list of bad words based on searches for insulting seeds. Then, based on word embeddings, they extend these linguistic resources to define bullying features, setting different weights to each feature based on the similarity between the word embeddings and concatenating them with bag-of-words features and latent semantic features to form a vector representation using word2vec. The insulting seeds list contains 350 words that indicate insult or negative emotions ("nigga", "bitch", "fuck", etc.). Using word embeddings, they verify the similarity between words ("beef" and "pork") through weights assigned to each one of them. When the final representation of each Internet message is obtained, the linear classifier SVM is used to detect the existence of cyberbullying.

The use of images to aid in cyberbullying detection is a complementary approach, given that by posting a photo, an individual may receive insults and provocations from people linked to him on social networks. Also, the publication of intimate photos by others to lead the person on the image to be humiliated in public is one of the concerns to consider in this type of study. Lightbody et al. [3] assure that combining sentiment analysis with image processing techniques is considered an appropriate platform for categorization of textual and visual connotations of content. With this, the authors intend to show that it is not only through text that the attack can be made, since the offensive text can be presented as an image, or else, the offence can be tried by editing a photo. They consider that the most relevant pictures will be those that may contain nudity, evidence of editing and analysis of text within the image. The existence of text related to the image helps to determine the risk of content negativity and the associated category.

Other work [14] intended to analyse the audio and text from Vine platform, as the popular social media sites are becoming increasingly visual, and the use of audio-based interfaces for interacting with both devices and other human beings is constantly growing. The authors believe that cyberbullying grows bigger and meaner with photos and videos, so they decided to collect features from the text, images and sounds of a Vine post such as number of words, sentiment, loudness or presence of drugs. The cognitive aspect of that analysis was related to the identified facial expressions in the images and to the evaluation of the semantic of comments and its similarity to previously identified cyberbullying situations. After detecting a positive case of bullying the objective is to send feedback to some stakeholders like parents or authorities, and trying to hide that from the general public, as they say that identifying individuals as both victims and bullies can have negative consequences, as the victims may be targeted for further bullying and identified bullies may face administrative or legal action.

As Instagram is one of the bigger photo-share social network, Housseinmardi et al. [11] did a manual labelling work for some of this application publications. They refer that cyberbullying on Instagram can happen in different ways, including posting a humiliating image of someone else by perhaps editing the image, posting mean or hateful comments, aggressive captions or hashtags, or creating fake profiles pretending to be someone else. They also consider the common psychological concerns in the available text and in the image content, so they can conclude that it is more probably to be facing a bullying situation when concerns like death or religion are found. Zhong et al. [15] want to look for some specific characteristics in Instagram bullied photos, such as skin tone or outdoor colours, for example, to check the possibility of racism or to find if photos at the beach are more susceptible.

4 Proposed Solution

Due to the increase of Internet usage, with special attention to the usage growth of online social platforms, we believe that action is needed regarding social aspects. More specifically, we want to address the bullying problem on online social platforms. The goal is to build a system to identify situations of cyberbullying autonomously and to adapt to new scenarios that may arise, learning over time and thereby increasing its effectiveness in each prediction for each analysed interaction in an online social network.

Online social networks are commonly used by young people, giving them the possibility to connect and interact with their friends. However, some of their connections can be more unfriendly and may start to execute some practices of bullying to attack someone when they feel anger, envy or jealous in relation to another individual. Knowing that most of the insulting content provided will be found in the form of text, this should be the focus of analysis to classify a situation as bullying or as not bullying.

In a previous work [16] we presented a model for a virtual social sensor that, by capturing the vast amount of public data available in online social platforms, analyses the behaviour of users in social networks. To achieve that, the virtual social sensor contains a set of modules, namely: natural language processing; emotion and sentiment detection; analysis of network interactions; and personality profiling based on the Big Five model [17]. Despite the original purpose of the sensor (being applied in smart environments and organisational applications contexts) with this work we want to endow the virtual social sensor with capabilities to respond to online social hazards.

Despite the virtual social sensor being equipped with a text analysis module, it is necessary to improve it to a point that, based on the similarity between the characteristics of phrases and words considered as offensive, indicates the probability of a new text belonging to each of the two classes mentioned (bullying or not bullying).

After researching about related works that were presented, we could choose to follow the approach to convert the textual content into word embeddings, which will represent it in the form of numerical vectors. That text, after being represented in the cartesian space, will allow us to find a measure of similarity between the different language resources through a Support Vector Machine that can output the final textual classification. However, performing only textual analysis to recognize a bullying situation will not be enough by itself to help reduce these situations in the future, even if the recidivism in practice of these acts can cause the social network to block or delete the aggressor account.

Since the sensor allows us to analyse the interactions in the network, it would be easy to verify what is the kind of people that a user usually interacts more frequently and in what way. For example, if an individual only tends to comment or exchange content with people of the same gender, and if it normally interacts in a way that provokes those people, the online social network may choose to avoid presenting people with a similar profile and personality, as well as not suggesting new connections to people who present these characteristics, in order to avoid scenarios that can lead to new situations of bullying. This may give us more information about the profile of people who are normally involved in a bullying situation, whether it is a victim or an aggressor, and in the same way that the sensor currently does to present content to the user based on their preferences, there could be an inverse process that would aim not to connect some kind people and some types of publications that could lead to a new bullying situation

There are other ways of practising bullying than just by text. One individual may share a picture of another to try to provoke embarrassment or to make him feel bad. This picture may even be accompanied by a description that further increases the level of aggressiveness of the situation, so another module can be coupled to the sensor to work in these tasks. Having the ability to look for the presence of people in the photos or videos that are usually shared over the different social networks may be an indicator that something is not right. If an image of another person is shared together with an offensive description, it is very likely that we are dealing with a case where someone is trying to threaten or denigrate the person in the picture.

To do this, we need to build a new module that can search for human presence in the images and, after finding them, step into a facial recognition task to know if the person in the image is the same one that shared it. In the case of being a different person who is present in this multimedia content, and the text that is placed in the description fits the patterns of a text characteristic of a bullying situation, the system should indicate this situation as such. This type of implementation will be simplified by the fact that there is several machine learning software available on the Internet that can perform this analysis with a high percentage of success, running its tasks in very short times, and can store the data of previous classifications to constantly improve its performance.

Often these images may contain text written on it due to graphical editions, which is a very common practice in social networks where you just can publish some update if you upload a photo, as the case of Instagram. That text could be the way the bully found to attack its target, even if the subject is not present in that photo. Additionally, some other components may be added to the photo, to make it look different from the reality, trying to embarrass someone. As result, we can also adapt this image analysis module to try to perform Optical Character Recognition tasks in order to convert the text in the image to plain text to be analyzed the same way we want to do with content description and comments.

One capability of the virtual social sensor is being able to identify traits of personality, further leading to the identification and clustering of profiles (based on personality). Since the personality is directly correlated to the behaviour expressed by someone, theoretically, it is possible to identify a bully or a potential situation of bullying before they are expressed. By being able to predict that someone can initiate a bullying situation, it is possible to engage with prevention measures before the hazard occurs, by monitoring users identified with potential bullies, or situations (like public communications) that can lead to a bullying situation.

In this type of cognitive analysis, we need to focus on the type of written text and its frequency, in the categories of posts the user normally interacts with and in the interests he or she may have and can be identified, for example, by the likes on a determined marketing or sports club page. With that, we will easily identify a pattern in user preferences and actions, so by his historical activity, it would be easier to predict if someone can be involved in a bullying scenario.

This solution can be directly implemented on the online social networks platforms to improve their services and stand out as good applications for young people share their interests.

5 Conclusion and Future Work

The constant growth of Internet usage and the services it provides is a result of the increasing commitment of thousands of millions of individuals across the globe. The new realities resulting from online platforms, specifically online social platforms, allow people to socialize and experience different realities, with the expense of some risks. Among those risks, we can find bullying, or cyberbullying, which can be prominent among children and can lead to more serious problems in their lives and having difficulties to be integrated into society.

The ability to identify and monitor these types of situations and identify the profiles of people who are most involved in bullying situations have been explored either by textual analysis or even by image recognition techniques. We believe that current approaches to this topic can be further improved by including a personality characteristic to the analysis.

Motivated by a previous model for a virtual social sensor, we can enhance the text analysis capabilities by including a module for detecting abusive sentences that can be classified as bullying. For the visual aspect, the development of a module capable of image recognition can work alongside the textual content present to enhance the prediction capabilities of possible social hazard situations. This prediction capability is further enhanced by the existing personality profiling module that, in combination with the described modules, can help the identification of new bullies by monitoring behaviour and analysing personality traits similarities with the profiles of known bullies.

As result, our next step is to develop the mentioned modules and work on a model solution for the identification, and categorization, of personality characteristics of bullies, or potential bullies. Since video content is also highly present on online social platforms, we will take into consideration the development and implementation of a sound/video recognition module that can help to identify physical and/or verbal situations of aggression. Implicitly, all this development is associated with a continuous process of data collection to be able to train each module.

References

1. Evans, C., Smokowski, P.: Theoretical explanations for bullying in school: how ecological processes propagate perpetration and victimization. University of Kansas, University of North Carolina, USA (2016)
2. Dinakar, K., Reichart, R., Lieberman, H.: Modeling the detection of textual cyberbullying. MIT Media Lab, Massachusetts Institute of Technology, Cambridge, USA (2011)

3. Lightbody, G., Bond, R., Mulvenna, M., Bi, Y., Mulligan, M.: Investigation into the automated detection of image based cyberbullying on social media platforms. School of Computing and Mathematics, University of Ulster, Northern Ireland. Carnbane Business Centre, Newry, Northern Ireland (2014)
4. Mascheroni, G., Cuman, A.: Net Children Go Mobile: Final Report. Educatt, Milano (2014)
5. McClowry, R., Miller, M., Mills, G.: Theoretical explanations for bullying in school: what family physicians can do to combat bullying. Department of Family and Community Medicine, Thomas Jefferson University, Philadelphia, USA (2017)
6. Hee, C., et al.: Automatic detection of cyberbullying in social media text. Ghent University, University of Antwerp, Belgium (2018)
7. Hardy, R., Norgaard, J.: Reputation in the internet black market: an empirical and theoretical analysis of the Deep Web. J. Inst. Econ. (2017). George Mason University, Virginia, USA
8. Patchin, J., Hinduja, S.: Digital self-harm among adolescents. University of Wisconsin-Eau Claire, Eau Claire, Wisconsin, USA. Florida Atlantic University, Jupiter, Florida, USA (2017)
9. The Next Web - "How Dangerous is Cyberbullying?". www.thenextweb-com/contributors/2017/10/04/how-dangerous-is-cyberbullying. Accessed 31 Oct 2017
10. Chatzakou, D., Kourtellis, N., Blackburn, J., Cristofaro, E., Strighini, G., Vakali, A.: Mean birds: detection aggression and bullying on Twitter. In: Proceedings of the 2017 ACM on Web Science Conference, pp. 13–22. ACM (2017)
11. Hosseinmardi, H., Mattson, S., Rafiq, R., Han, R., Lv, Q., Mishra, S.: Analyzing labeled cyberbullying incidents on the Instagram social networks. University of Colorado Boulder, Boulder, USA (2015)
12. Huang, K., Singh, V., Atrey, P.: Cyber Bullying Detection Using Social and Textual Analysis. ACM, New York (2014)
13. Zhao, R., Zhou, A., Mao, K.: Automatic detection of cyberbullying on social networks based on bullying features. School of Electrical and Electronic Engineering, Nanyang Technological University, Singapore (2016)
14. Soni, S., Singh, V.: See No Evil, Hear No Evil: Audio-Visual-Textual Cyberbullying Detection. Rutgers University, New Brunswick (2018)
15. Zhong, H., et al.: Content-driven detection of cyberbullying on the Instagram social network. In: IJCAI, pp. 3952–3958 (2016)
16. Barbosa, R., Santos, R.: Online social networks as sensors in smart environments. CIICESI, ESTGF, IPP School of Technology and Management of Felgueiras, Felgueiras, Portugal (2016)
17. Ghavami, S., Asadpour, M., Mahdavi, M.: Facebook user's like behavior can reveal personality. In: 2015 7th Conference on Information and Technology (IKT), Urmia, pp. 1–3 (2015)

Exploring Novel Methodology
for Classifying Cognitive Workload

Seth Siriya[1]([⊠]) [iD], Martin Lochner[2] [iD], Andreas Duenser[2] [iD],
and Ronnie Taib[3] [iD]

[1] University of Melbourne, Melbourne, Australia
`ssiriya@student.unimelb.edu.au`
[2] Data61, CSIRO, Hobart, Australia
[3] Data61, CSIRO, Eveleigh, Australia

Abstract. This paper describes our work in extracting useful cognitive
load classification information from a relatively simple and non-invasive
physiological measurement technique, with application in a range of
Human Factors and Human-Computer Interaction contexts. We employ
novel methodologies, including signal processing, machine learning and
genetic algorithms, to classify Galvanic Skin Response/Electrodermal
Activity (GSR/EDA) signals during performance of a customised game
task (*UAV Defender*) in high- and low-workload conditions. Our results
reveal that Support Vector Machine Linear was the most successful
technique for classifying the level of cognitive load that an operator is
undergoing during easy, medium, and difficult operation conditions. This
methodology has the advantage of applicability in *critical task* situations,
where other cognitive load measurement methodologies are problematic
due to sampling delay (e.g. questionnaires), or difficulty of implementation (e.g. other psych-physiological measures). A proposed cognitive load
classification pipeline for real-time implementation and its use in human
factors contexts is discussed.

Keywords: Cognitive load · Galvanic Skin Response ·
Electrodermal Activity · Psycho-physiology · Analytics ·
Machine learning · Decision response task

1 Introduction

When operating complex machinery, dealing with sensitive control apparatus,
or navigating vehicles of any size, it is increasingly evident that the level of cognitive load (CL) the operator is incurring has a direct impact on the operator's
performance on the task, (e.g. [12]). Likewise, such multi-tasking during critical
task operation has detrimental effects on both the primary task (e.g. driving)
and secondary task performance [5,13].

Managing cognitive load promises to optimise the way information is processed and responded to by humans, addressing errors due to overload, which

P. Cortez et al. (Eds.): INTETAIN 2018, LNICST 273, pp. 105–114, 2019.
https://doi.org/10.1007/978-3-030-16447-8_11

was identified as a factor in the tragic crash of flight AF447 in 2009 [6], or conversely to underload, in typical surveillance scenarios where an operator must be able to detect minute anomalies in very long sequences of otherwise normal observations.

Where our current work has useful, and indeed extremely relevant scope given recent and expected technological advances, is in the domain of applied, mission-critical environments. In this context, we define a critical task as one that: (a) needs active and substantial attentional resources for its successful execution, and (b) could result (or will likely result) in catastrophic circumstances, i.e. injury, death, or damage to property, in the event of task failure. While the large body of existing laboratory evidence is useful in understanding CL, and predicting the effects of high and low workload tasks, there remains a gap in our ability to monitor this phenomenon in the actual operating environments where it is arguably most important. In addition to affording new ways of monitoring CL in real-time and measuring or evaluating operator performance and interaction with systems, psycho-physiological measures such as those described in this paper can contribute to the development of novel, real-time, direct and indirect human-computer interaction (HCI) techniques (e.g. [18,19]).

2   Related Work

Cognitive load corresponds to the mental effort expended carrying out a task, based on the premise that working memory capacity is a limited resource in the human cognitive system, yet is critical in coordinating memory, attention and perception [2].

By measuring the cognitive load experienced by a user, applications could adapt the amount and pace of content they provide to continuously optimise delivery, hence maximising the throughput of information between the human and computer. From the literature, we can identify four broad ways to measure cognitive load: subjective assessment methods, performance based techniques, behavioural measurements, and psycho-physiological measurements. We here focus on the latter.

Psycho-physiological measurements use changes in a person's physiological state to infer a change in mental state - in this case, cognitive workload. There are numerous examples of such measures, including direct measures of brain activity (EEG, FNIR; e.g. [1,7]), ocular activity (e.g., [19]), breath rate, heart rate speed and variability [23]. For a detailed review, please see [3].

In this paper, we focus on one of the oldest and most studied measures of human psycho-physiology: Galvanic Skin Response, also known as Electrodermal Activity. Whereas most of the above techniques require expensive apparatus, considerable time for set-up, and specific laboratory techniques for data collection, the GSR is of minimal complexity, requiring only two proximally-located electrodes in contact with the epidermis. The metric itself is simply the electrical conductance between these two points, as measured in microsiemens. Whereas historically the raw value of the GSR has been of primary interest, we present here some novel methodologies for usefully classifying these signals under different CL conditions.

Early work on GSR discriminated between tonic (baseline level, also known as skin conductance level) and phasic (fluctuations due to physiology activity, also known as skin conductance responses) GSR [11]. On the other hand, a study into driver stress simply smoothed the GSR signal with a digital elliptical filter cutting at 4 Hz, and then used slope characteristics (magnitude and durations) as features [8]. Another study specifically targeting CL measurement from GSR showed that a simple, unimodal metric such as *accumulated GSR* can be a reasonable indicator of CL [20]. Other research has shown that GSR can be a good indicator of the quality of human decisions. In this work the raw signal was first smoothed using a Hann window function, followed by z-standardisation before applying extrema-based and statistic-based features similar to the above studies [24]. Finally, some other studies have explored the applicability of feature extraction methods used for other signals to GSR. For example, EEG and EMG methods have been included for analysis in this investigation [9,15].

3   Methodology

45 Participants (ages 21–35) from a University research pool were involved in this study. They were paid 40USD for completing two 1-hour test sessions. Participants reported having normal or corrected-to-normal visual acuity.

Participants completed a computer-based task, UAV Defender, over two testing sessions. The task was developed at the Tasmanian Cognition Lab (University of Tasmania) and was carried out on standard current-model Windows desktop computers, and standard peripheral devices. The GSR signal was collected from the finger and thumb of the non-dominant hand, using commercially available Neulog GSR logger-sensors. GSR data was collected at 20 Hz. The ISO Decision Response Task [10] was implemented using the DRT kit available from RED Scientific (USA), using the haptic-buzzer stimulus setup, with the buzzer located at the left collar-bone, and a foot switch for reaction time (RT) responses.

The UAV Defender task requires participants to track multiple UAVs as they traverse a landscape, as viewed from a *birds-eye* viewpoint, i.e., from directly overhead. Similar in implementation to the Multiple Object Tracking task [17], we manipulated difficulty in three levels by requiring all participants to track either 3, 5 or 7 targets simultaneously. The level of difficulty was fully counterbalanced across trials. Participants were required to click on a UAV when a visible fuel level marker became low, as indicated by a colour bar on the UAV icon. Trials of UAV Defender lasted 2 min each, and participants completed 24 trials on two consecutive testing days, for a total of 48 trials (with random counterbalanced sequence of difficulty levels).

Data Cleaning. Of the initial 46 participants in this experiment, one participant was dropped completely due to an intermittent short in the GSR signal. For the remaining 45 participants, we implemented a data cleaning procedure to remove trials in which more than half of the trial data exceeded specific cut-off limits. High cut-off was $9.9\,\mu S$, and the low cut-off was $1\,\mu S$.

Metrics. While much of the past research into GSR and workload has generally studied the raw GSR signal (i.e. skin conductance), we have attempted here to develop a suite of metrics that are intended to increase our ability to differentiate high-workload GSR signals from low-workload GSR signals. These include both successful metrics from recently published work, and novel experimental metrics.

Standardized GSR and Accumulated GSR: Previously employed with success in [14], z-score standardization of the GSR signal has been shown to improve discriminability between workload levels. Accumulated GSR is the sum of raw signal values in a trial, which has been found as descriptive of CL [14].

Slope, or Gradient of the GSR Signal: Novel to our present analysis, this metric takes the gradient, or slope, of the GSR signal by taking the line of best fit over a rolling window of 40 samples (i.e. 2 s of data at 20 Hz). This methodology enables us to remove the overall drift component of the raw GSR signal, and smooth out high-frequency signal while retaining some local information, with a score of zero indicating no change in the GSR signal.

Zero Crossings: The rate of 'zero crossings', measures the rate at which the gradient changes from positive to negative. This metric enables us to assess the *speed* of the waveform without resorting to Fourier analysis such as the Fast Fourier Transform (FFT) or the Discrete Fourier Transform (DFT).

Negative Slope Percentage: Negative Slope Percentage (NSP) measures the proportion of time within a trial that the slope of the raw GSR signal is below zero, indicating a decline in skin conductance. This was an exploratory feature testing the hypothesis that decreased load results in decreasing skin conductance.

PSD Coefficients: Power Spectral Density (PSD) coefficients are descriptive of how important a frequency is for a signal. We used Welch's method to obtain the coefficients, since it allows control of the variance of the estimate (at the cost of frequency resolution) [22]. The spectrum for GSR is concentrated below 0.5 Hz [16], therefore we only analyse coefficients within this range. Then segpoints is defined as the number of PSD coefficients located between 0 and 0.5 Hz. Segpoints values that were investigated were 10, 20, 30, 40, 50 and 60. PSD coefficients were obtained from the Standardised GSR and slope.

Hjorth Parameters: We extracted the Hjorth parameters (which were developed for EEG analysis) from both the Standardised GSR and Slope of the GSR signal [9]. The parameters were extracted as features for both the Standardised GSR and the slope.

EMG-Based Metrics: Alongside the Hjorth parameters which were selected due to their success in EEG analysis, we also explored EMG-based features due to their usage of frequency-domain information. These were the first, second and third spectral moments, mean frequency, peak frequency and total power [15]. Again, features were extracted for both the Standardised GSR and slope.

Feature Exploration. To determine how descriptive these features are of cognitive load, we performed a one-way within-subject ANOVA test for each of the metrics on day one, with game difficulty level as the independent variable. We applied within-subject standardisation for the features to account for between subject differences. This is similar to feature calibration previously applied in CL classification research, but with z-score standardisation rather than divide-by-mean calibration due to the mean of some features being zero [14].

Classification Model. Following the analysis of features, we generated various classification models and evaluated their performance.

Model Selection, Training and Testing: The purpose of model selection is to find features (with within-subject standardisation) and parameters best suited to the problem of classifying CL. This was repeated on both days individually to get a unique set of features and model parameters corresponding to day one and day two. Model training was repeated for both days, such that a model was trained using parameters and features from day one, and repeating this separately for day two. Finally, models we trained on day one data are tested on day two data, and vice-versa. The purpose of testing on the opposite dataset is to observe how well models generalise to unseen data [4]. Model performance was measured using F1-Score.

Genetic Algorithm-based Feature Selection: The goal of feature selection during model selection is to find the best subset of features that are informative of CL levels. Since it would take a long time for an exhaustive search through all possible combinations of features, we applied genetic algorithm-based search to explore the feature space for each segpoints value.

Two classification algorithms were used in model selection: Naïve Bayes and K-Nearest Neighbours. Fitness scores were calculated via leave-one-subject-out cross validation [14]. We implemented a genetic algorithm in Python using the DEAP evolutionary computation framework, with most parameters replicated from previous work [21]. The sole exception was probability of mutation, which we increased to 0.01 due to the smaller feature space. Finally, we used three different learning algorithms for the model training/testing stages: K-Nearest Neighbours, Random Forest and Support Vector Machines (SVM) Linear.

4   Results

4.1   Feature Exploration

Generating PSD with multiple segpoints is computationally expensive and each PSD represents similar information (with slight differences due to variance-resolution trade-off). Therefore the best segpoints value should be determined. We approached this from the perspective of determining the segpoints value with the most number of significant features. Following ANOVA testing on all of the features, we counted the number of significant frequency-domain features for each segpoints, which is recorded in Fig. 1.

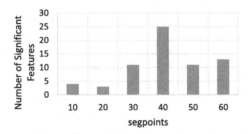

Fig. 1. Comparison of number of significant frequency domain features generated from PSD of varying segpoints

We also compared the individual features themselves using ANOVA to gain insight into specific measures which are characteristic of CL. Of the time domain features, Hjorth complexity of the sloped signal had the highest effect size $(F(2,66) = 9.50, p < .01, \eta^2 = .13)$. In the frequency domain, the mean frequency of the slope $(segpoints = 10)$ was found to have the highest value $(F(2,66) = 13.88, p < .01, \eta^2 = .17)$. Of the frequency domain features extracted from the PSD for $segpoints = 40$, the PSD coefficient at 0.065 Hz had the highest value $(F(2,66) = 9.53, p < .01, \eta^2 = .13))$. For comparison, the effect size of Accumulated GSR, which was previously found to be informative of CL [14], was also measured $(F(2,66) = 4.32, p = 0.017, \eta^2 = .061))$.

4.2 Classification Model

The F1-Scores from leave-one-subject-out validation during model selection were recorded for both days and are shown in Fig. 2. Note that only the results using the K-Nearest Neighbour algorithm for fitness evaluation is shown, since Naïve Bayes performed at the level of a random classifier. The graphs demonstrate the segpoints values that had the best F1-Score (and thus were chosen for the model on each day). These were segpoints = 40 on day one (F1-Score = 0.406) and segpoints = 30 on day two (F1-Score = 0.434).

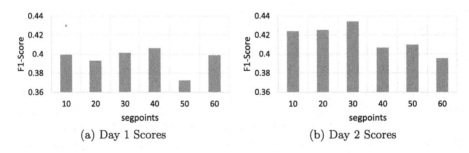

(a) Day 1 Scores   (b) Day 2 Scores

Fig. 2. Comparison of F1-Scores for varying segpoints in model selection stage on day one (a) and day two (b) using genetic algorithm-based feature selection

The results from the model testing stage are shown in Fig. 3, comparing the performance of the models trained/ tested using K-Nearest Neighbours, Random Forest and SVM Linear, alongside the Random Baseline performance and a model generated using Accumulated GSR for comparison (with Random Forest as learning algorithm since it performed best in combination with Accumulated GSR). SVM Linear had the best performance across both tests. The model trained on day one and tested on day two had an F1-Score of 0.365, and the model trained on day two and tested on day one had an F1-Score of 0.3774.

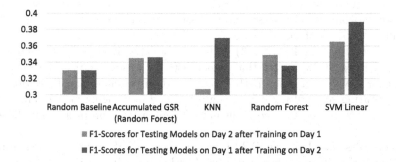

Fig. 3. Comparison of F1-Scores across different algorithms in model testing stage using genetic algorithm-based feature selection

5   Discussion

Our results for effect size during feature exploration indicate that Mean frequency of slope (segpoints = 10), PSD coefficients of slope at 0.065 Hz (segpoints = 40) and Hjorth complexity of slope were more discriminative between CL levels compared to Accumulated GSR, a feature used in previous work [14]. This suggests that, at least for our data, which is based on a multiple object tracking task as compared to solving arithmetic tasks, these new metrics may better characterise different CL levels.

When comparing segpoints, setting segpoints to 40 on day one maximised number of significant frequency domain features. Setting segpoints allows selection of trade-off between variance and frequency resolution of the PSD, so segpoints = 40 could represent a good trade-off for feature extraction from the PSD.

However, more significant features associated with a segpoints, does not necessarily mean that the features generated for the segpoints are more informative of CL. Note that even though segpoints = 40 had the greatest number of significant features, mean frequency for segpoints = 10 had the highest effect size. This suggests that there may be individual features for specific segpoints that are highly indicative of CL, even though they may contain fewer significant features. The obvious limitation of this analysis approach is that it does not take the effect of using multiple features as an indication of CL into consideration. This is addressed through the analysis of the classification models.

The model selection results from the genetic algorithm-based feature selection (Fig. 2) provide some insight into an appropriate segpoints value for generating the PSD coefficients. We found that *segpoints* = 40 and 30 were the best performing values in both day one and two. Note that the range of segpoints values tested was 10 to 60 with increments of 10, and so the model selection results suggests that a mid-range trade-off (given the sampling frequency of 20 Hz and recorded duration of 2 min) sets the best frame size and trade-off between frequency resolution and estimate variance. Such a result agrees with the analysis from the feature exploration section, where *segpoints* = 40 had the most number of significant features.

Model testing results (Fig. 3) indicate the effectiveness of the approach towards generating a model that generalises to unseen data. The classifiers (except for KNN) performed better than Random Baseline, and therefore seem to be capturing some of the effect (cognitive load influencing GSR). The inconsistency of KNN could be a consequence of being an inappropriate classification mechanism.

The results also show the SVM Linear models had the highest scores in both tests, suggesting it generalises the best. Furthermore, it consistently performed better than Accumulated GSR models, such that combining multiple relevant features using SVM Linear is better than solely relying on Accumulated GSR. However, performance still left much to be desired, with F1-scores slightly below 0.4 on three-class classification during testing. Perhaps the measured signal was externally influenced by factors aside from CL, or the features and classifier were not the most suitable choices for capturing the effect. Also, the features were not optimised for the classifier (due to computational limitations), since KNN was used for feature selection and SVM Linear for training/testing.

6   Conclusions

In this study we have conducted an investigation into classification techniques for human cognitive workload using Galvanic Skin Response, when performing a modified multiple object tracking task, *UAV Defender*, over two consecutive days of testing. The current methodology has been shown to outperform previously used metrics, and provide moderate discriminability for CL between levels of task difficulty, although the effects described herein leave room for improvement. These results are encouraging and provide justification for further research, including implementing the current methodology on new data sets, as well as testing other GSR devices (as there is some question of fidelity with the low-cost GSR sensors employed here). While affordability is a key aspect of our proposed system, we need to maximise the quality of the original GSR signal to promote the most accurate level of classification possible.

One of the goals of this research is to develop *lightweight classification systems* for use in critical task environments, where traditional means of workload detection, and more complex psychophysiology-based measures are unsuitable (e.g. environments such as road transportation, maritime transportation, operation of heavy machinery, etc.). We believe that the combination of low-cost equipment, reliable and relatively non-invasive sensors, and sophisticated data processing techniques will allow us to monitor CL in critical task environments as well as in the rising field of human-in-the-loop autonomous systems, where monitoring of autonomous systems is necessary.

Although a real-time system could be designed based on our analysis pipeline, there are some considerations that need to be taken into account. The feature extraction we used in this study occurred on signals using a 2-min time window. In practice, this would mean a long delay for changes in CL to be measured.

Further, due to the size of our sampling population, we applied within-subject standardisation in our analysis for both GSR signals and features. This implies that a deployed system would work in a user-dependent fashion, with every user having to perform a training phase. However, training the model with a larger pool of participants is likely to generate generalisable models that would perform well on new target users. This will be part of future work.

Acknowledgements. This research was funded in part by the CSIRO Data61 Automation Trust and Workload CRP, and Australian Research Council DP160101891, CERA247.

References

1. Ayaz, H., et al.: Cognitive workload assessment of air traffic controllers using optical brain imaging sensors. In: Rice, V. (ed.) Advances in Understanding Human Performance, vol. 20105280, pp. 21–31. CRC Press, Boca Raton (2010)
2. Baddeley, A.D.: Working memory. Science **255**(556–559), 5044 (1992)
3. Cain, B.: A review of the mental workload literature. Technical report, DTIC (2007). http://oai.dtic.mil/oai/oai?verb=getRecord&metadataPrefix=html&identifier=ADA474193
4. Cawley, G.C., Talbot, N.L.: On over-fitting in model selection and subsequent selection bias in performance evaluation. J. Mach. Learn. Res. **11**(Jul), 2079–2107 (2010)
5. Dünser, A., Mancero, G.: The use of depth in change detection and multiple object tracking. Ergon. Open J. **2**, 142–149 (2009)
6. Bureau d'Enquetes et d'Analyses France (BEA): Final Report: Accident to Airbus A330–203 Registered F-GZCP, Air France AF 447 Rio de Janeiro - Paris, 1st June 2009. Technical report, Air Accident Investigation Unit (AAIU), October 2014. http://www.aaiu.ie/node/687
7. Funke, G., et al.: Evaluation of subjective and EEG-based measures of mental workload. In: Stephanidis, C. (ed.) HCI 2013. CCIS, vol. 373, pp. 412–416. Springer, Heidelberg (2013). https://doi.org/10.1007/978-3-642-39473-7_82
8. Healey, J., Picard, R.: SmartCar: detecting driver stress. In: Proceedings 15th International Conference on Pattern Recognition, ICPR-2000, vol. 4, pp. 218–221 (2000)
9. Hjorth, B.: EEG analysis based on time domain properties. Electroencephalogr. Clin. Neurophysiol. **29**(3), 306–310 (1970)

10. International Organization for Standardization: ISO 17488:2016(en), Road vehicles - transport information and control systems - detection-response task (DRT) for assessing attentional effects of cognitive load in driving. Technical Report ISO 17488:2016(en), International (2016)
11. Lim, C.L., et al.: Decomposing skin conductance into tonic and phasic components. Int. J. Psychophysiol. **25**(2), 97–109 (1997)
12. Lochner, M., Duenser, A., Lutzhoft, M., Brooks, B., Rozado, D.: Analysis of maritime team workload and communication dynamics in standard and emergency scenarios. J. Shipp. Trade **3**(1), 2 (2018)
13. Lochner, M.J., Trick, L.M.: Multiple-object tracking while driving: the multiple-vehicle tracking task. Atten. Percept. Psychophys. **76**, 2326–2345 (2014)
14. Nourbakhsh, N., Wang, Y., Chen, F.: GSR and blink features for cognitive load classification. In: Kotzé, P., Marsden, G., Lindgaard, G., Wesson, J., Winckler, M. (eds.) INTERACT 2013. LNCS, vol. 8117, pp. 159–166. Springer, Heidelberg (2013). https://doi.org/10.1007/978-3-642-40483-2_11
15. Phinyomark, A., Thongpanja, S., Hu, H., Phukpattaranont, P., Limsakul, C.: The usefulness of mean and median frequencies in electromyography analysis. In: Naik, G.R. (ed.) Computational Intelligence in Electromyography Analysis - A Perspective on Current Applications and Future Challenges. INTECH Open Access Publisher (2012). https://doi.org/10.5772/50639
16. Posada-Quintero, H.F., Chon, K.H.: Frequency-domain electrodermal activity index of sympathetic function. In: 2016 IEEE-EMBS International Conference on Biomedical and Health Informatics (BHI), pp. 497–500, Febraury 2016
17. Pylyshyn, Z.W., Storm, R.W.: Tracking multiple independent targets: evidence for a parallel tracking mechanism. Spat. Vis. **3**(3), 179–197 (1988)
18. Rozado, D., Duenser, A.: Combining EEG with pupillometry to improve cognitive workload detection. IEEE Comput. **48**(10), 18–25 (2015)
19. Rozado, D., Lochner, M., Engelke, U., Duenser, A.: Detecting intention through motor-imagery-triggered pupil dilations. Hum.-Comput. Inter., 1–31, Febraury 2017
20. Shi, Y., Ruiz, N., Taib, R., Choi, E., Chen, F.: Galvanic skin response (GSR) as an index of cognitive load. In: CHI 2007 Extended Abstracts, pp. 2651–2656. ACM, New York, April 2007
21. Uguz, H.: A two-stage feature selection method for text categorization by using information gain, principal component analysis and genetic algorithm. Knowl.-Based Syst. **24**(7), 1024–1032 (2011)
22. Welch, P.: The use of fast Fourier transform for the estimation of power spectra: a method based on time averaging over short, modified periodograms. IEEE Trans. Audio Electroacoust. **15**(2), 70–73 (1967)
23. Wilson, G.F., Fullenkamp, P., Davis, I.: Evoked potential, cardiac, blink, and respiration measures of pilot workload in air-to-ground missions. Aviat. Space Environ. Med. **65**(2), 100–105 (1994)
24. Zhou, J., Sun, J., Chen, F., Wang, Y., Taib, R., Khawaji, A., Li, Z.: Measurable decision making with GSR and pupillary analysis for intelligent user interface. ACM Trans. Comput.-Hum. Interact. **21**(6), 1–23 (2015)

Virtual Environments, Entertainment and Games

Scene Reconstruction for Storytelling in 360° Videos

Gonçalo Pinheiro[1]([✉]), Nelson Alves[1], Luis Magalhães[2], Luís Agrellos[3], and Miguel Guevara[1]

[1] Centro de Computação Gráfica,
Campus de Azurém, Edifício 14, 4800-058 Guimarães, Portugal
`goncalo.pinheiro@ccg.pt`
[2] University of Minho, Campus de Azurém, 4800-058 Guimarães, Portugal
[3] GMK, Cais das Pedras n°08, 4050-465 Porto, Portugal

Abstract. In immersive and interactive contents like 360-degrees videos the user has the control of the camera, which poses a challenge to the content producer since the user may look to where he wants. This paper presents the concept and first steps towards the development of a framework that provides a workflow for storytelling in 360-degrees videos. With the proposed framework it will be possible to connect a sound to a source and taking advantage of binaural audio it will help to redirect the user attention to where the content producer wants. To present this kind of audio, the scenario must be mapped/reconstructed so as to understand how the objects contained in it interfere with the sound waves propagation. The proposed system is capable of reconstructing the scenario from a stereoscopic, still or motion 360-degrees video when provided in an equirectangular projection. The system also incorporates a module that detects and tracks people, mapping their motion from the real world to the 3D world. In this document we describe all the technical decisions and implementations of the system. To the best of our knowledge, this system is the only that has shown the capability to reconstruct scenarios in a large variety of 360 footage and allows for the creation of binaural audio from that reconstruction.

Keywords: 360 videos · Storytelling · Scene Reconstruction ·
Binaural sound · Computer vision · Computer graphics ·
3D reconstruction · People detection · People tracking

1 Introduction

With the rising popularity and accessibility of 360-degrees cameras, 360-degrees movies are bound to become increasingly common. Contrary to regular footage films, the director has no control as to where the spectator is looking. The action can occur while the viewer is unaware, as such a solution that redirects the spectator's attention without explicitly telling him where to look and maintaining the

P. Cortez et al. (Eds.): INTETAIN 2018, LNICST 273, pp. 117–126, 2019.
https://doi.org/10.1007/978-3-030-16447-8_12

in-scenario abstraction must be developed. To address this problem we propose the creation of binaural audio from conventional audio sources.

The use of binaural sound is described as good solution [10] but in order to be able to use it we must reconstruct all planes contained in the scene for modelling the room acoustics.

Focusing in this exact problem is the S3A spatial audio team proposing [14] where they present a block world reconstruction, from 360-degree stereo images, proving that planes and their materials are enough to render accurate spatial audio [15]. We follow the previously presented approach and simplify the process by estimating only the planes presented in the scene.

Persons are one important sound source on videos and usually are in motion. Since we intend to reconstruct the scenario and use binaural sound it makes sense to track persons in order to get their trajectory in the 360° video. Thus, we aim for a recording trajectories, which provides the system with the ability to associate a sound source to a person. This allows to take their motion into consideration when rendering the audio.

Our system's end goal is to provide the editor with the tools necessary to create binaural sound for arbitrary 360° videos. This toolkit will integrate a video editing software, as an add-on or pluggin, to take advantage from the editor's experience in their preferred software.

In this paper existing solutions for 3D reconstruction and people detection and tracking are reviewed and we present the initial thoughts and rough sketches of our system.

2   Related Work

Related to our work are the approaches that reconstruct scenarios, detect and track persons from videos or images. As such, a brief overview of the state of the art in 3D reconstruction, person detection and tracking is presented.

2.1   3D Scene Reconstruction

The 3D reconstruction of real objects or scenes is a topic that falls in the computer vision field. For that purpose, there are several algorithms and techniques in the literature that are highly dependent on the specific scenario of application. In the context of this work, it is important to understand the type of footage that can be fed to the system: (1) Single vs Stereo Videos - single perspective vs two records with a fixed baseline between the cameras and (2) Camera Motion: the camera may be still or in motion;

Stereo Reconstruction. A system capable of generating accurate dense 3d reconstructions from stereo sequences was developed by Geiger et al. [9]. This reconstruction pipeline combines a sparse feature matcher in conjunction with a robust visual odometry algorithm with efficient stereo matching and a multi-view linking scheme for generating consistent 3d point clouds. Kim and Hilton

[14] propose a block world reconstruction from spherical stereo image pairs. Before reconstructing, the spherical image is converted to a cubic projection for an easier facade alignment. Regions are also segmented in order to identify and reconstruct planes.

Structure from Motion. Several methods have been presented using structure from motion in tasks of reconstruction from moving videos [19,24,25,28]. Structure from motion has also been applied to 360 videos [29]. Some approaches refine the structure from motion using bundle adjustment for an accurate reconstruction [21,27]. Other processes also filter the reconstruction with a priori information and/or geographic references [3,21,30].

Simultaneous localization and mapping (SLAM) has also been used on reconstruction tasks in motion footage [13,32] and proved to work well in populated environments [20].

Depth Estimation from Single Image. When trying to reconstruct the scenario of a video with no camera motion the challenge is in the depth estimation task since it is impossible to triangulate the position of each pixel from different perspectives.

Using conventional computer vision techniques some methods were developed to estimate depth from single images or static videos and a posteriori reconstruct the scenario. Liu et al. [17] performed a semantic segmentation of the scene. Given the semantic context of the scene, depth is estimated considering a pixel or super-pixel at a time. Zhuo et al. [33] developed a method to estimate the structure of an indoor scenario from a single image. Local depth is estimated creating super-pixels for an easier extraction of uniform planes.

Some approaches have been made using deep learning and convolutional neural networks. Eigen et al. [7] presented a system capable of generate a depth map from a single image using two CNN's. The first estimates depth at general level and the second one does the estimation locally. Ewerth et al. [8] combined monocular depth clues and feature extraction feeding it to a ranking model. Chen et al. [6] used a RGB-D dataset and created a new dataset with the closest and farthest planes labelled to train an auto-encoder CNN to generate a depth map.

2.2   Person Detection and Tracking

The ability of detecting and tracking persons in videos, has long been of interest for the computer vision community specially driven by the automatic visual surveillance goal. Following, are some of the more relevant approaches described in the literature.

Using Conventional Computer Vision. Andriluka et al. [4] firstly detect pedestrians in real-world scenes using an object detection model that doesn't consider any temporal constraints. To provide hypotheses for the position they propose a kinematic limb model. This grants the system expressiveness and robustness which reduces the number of false positives and facilitates detecting people in crowded scenes. Breuers et al. [5] developed three modules for addressing this problem in RGB-D images. The detection is made based on depth templates of upper bodies while the tracking is made using the MDL-tracker described by [12]. The third module is responsible for analyzing the head orientation and skeleton pose.

Using Deep Learning. Lin et al. [16] developed RetinaNet, a CNN for object and person detection. RetinaNet is composed by two sub networks, one responsible for feature extraction and one responsible for classification and drawing the bounding box. Tome et al. [26] reconstruct the 3D human pose from a single RGB image and the 2D joint estimation through a multi-stage CNN architecture. Guler et al. [11] mapped all pixels belonging to a person in a video using CNNs. Firstly, the whole body is estimated using classification and regression. After each body part is then located and a mesh drawn in all body pixels. Stewart et al. [23] present a new loss function which is applied to a classifier in order to identify the candidate bounding boxes of extracted representation generated by a CNN layer. Spinnelo et al. [22] uses AdaBoost for people classification training on acquired data considering that the appearance of people is highly variable. Instead of trying to segment the body in the different parts the detected body is segmented by height creating independent classifiers for each-one. Zhang et al. [31] presents a network for joint human detection and head pose estimation from rgb-d videos.

3   System Architecture

The system can be summed into five main modules presented in Fig. 1. Through analyzing an input video file, our system will allow for an editor to associate different sounds with their respective sources.

The first module is responsible for video pre-processing. The goal is to prepare the video to the subsequent processing steps. An example of a pre-processing method is to undistort the 360 video, from an equirectangular, fisheye or dual-fisheye format, to provide the next module with a standard video in an interpretable format for the computer vision methods that will be applied. This module is also capable of determining if the camera is moving or still which will determine the method used for reconstructing the footage.

The objective of the second module is to reconstruct the 3D model of a scene. For this purpose were identified three scenarios. If the camera is moving, it is possible to construct the point cloud using Structure from Motion techniques. In case of a still camera, depth has to be inferred before constructing the point cloud. In the stereoscopy case, depth of each feature point can be estimated due to the different perspectives of the scenario. In any case, a point cloud is created from which planes are extracted and the mesh of the scenario is generated.

Working in parallel with the 3D reconstruction module, the detection and tracking module is responsible for mapping the motion of the tracked persons into the generated spatial reconstruction. The trajectory will be represented by equally spaced points generating an approximation of the movement. In order to free the system from heavy processing the sound will only be mapped from a selected subset of all points identified. The goal is to automatically associate speech or sound to the detected person and regardless of their movement, the sound will always seem to follow its source.

The plane segmentation module will identify the main flat surfaces in the point cloud, generated by the reconstruction, which are the most significant for simulating acoustics.

The storyteller module will be responsible for the user interface, since it will have access to the results of all previous stages. Additionally, it is at this stage that the binaural sound is effectively rendered.

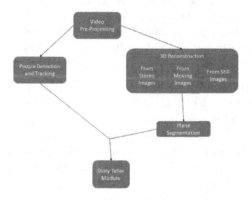

Fig. 1. System architecture

In following sections we specify all technical decisions made to date while developing the system.

3.1 Pre-processing

Motion Detection. Before reconstructing the scenario contained in a video it is necessary to understand the camera motion. This will decide which reconstruction method it's possible to apply.

For this task the Lucas-Kanade method for optical flow estimation was considered. This motion estimation is calculated frame by frame. Features are detected and distances are calculated between them in consecutive frames. Movement is assumed if the distance of a particular pair of features is bigger than one pixel. We consider that a whole frame is moving if most of the features are moving too.

360 Unwrapping. In order to make the video interpretable for the next steps, more specifically to the detection and tracking module it's necessary to remove the distortion contained in each frame.

From the 360-degree video, frame views are rendered at a specific vertical and horizontal field of view and resolution from an image in equirectangular projection using the software provided by [1].

3.2   Reconstruction

Motion. From videos where the camera is moving it is possible to reconstruct the scene by applying structure from motion. VisualSFM is being used to accomplish this task. Due to the fact that we are not performing keyframe selection, the computation is naturally heavier.

Still Camera. To reconstruct the scenario from a video with no camera motion we are using the PlaneNet DNN proposed by Liu et al. [18]. This system is capable of reconstructing planes from a single image which can be compared to reconstructing from a frame of a video filmed with a still camera.

Stereo. Using stereo footage we have two perspectives of the same scenario, so it is possible to infer the depth of each pixel by creating a disparity map.

Disparity maps were created using block matching algorithm, the Semi-Global Block Matching Stereo Correspondence Algorithm, the Stereo Belief Propagation and the Stereo Constant Space Belief Propagation. Visually, the Stereo Constant Space Belief Propagation algorithm performed better when compared to the others methods.

Having the disparity map and the camera's intrinsic parameters, it is possible to re-project that disparity to 3D space using the OpenCV library.

3.3   Person Detection and Tracking

Detection. The detection phase has the goal of giving the initial bounding box to the tracking algorithm as we try to automate the whole detection and tracking process. This process is made using the RetinaNet proposed by Lin et al. [16]. For each detected person a bounding box is generated.

Tracking. Having the RetinaNet bounding box we resize it to 20% of the original size to guarantee that the pixels inside of the bounding box belong exclusively to the tracked person. To accomplish this task we tested several algorithms like BOOSTING, Multiple Instance Learning (MIL), Kernelized Correlation Filters, tracking, learning and detection, MEDIANFLOW, GOTURN, MOSSE and the Discriminative Correlation Filter with Channel and Spatial Reliability (DCF-CSR). In our testing samples the DCF-CSR algorithm was the most robust under different light conditions and re-tracking occluded persons.

4   Preliminary Results

In this section we present the results of the work realized to date. All the results described were measured qualitatively with direct observation.

The system is already able to detect if there is any camera motion, showing some instability when performing this task on a video with a moving crowd. In addition, vertical and horizontal stereoscopy are also identified.

The 360 unwarpping proved to work well when removing the distortion from a frame. In Fig. 2 it is presented the full 360° frame. The Fig. 3 is rendered at the center of the original frame and the Fig. 4 at 90°. It is possible to observe that both figures present no distortion.

Fig. 2. 360-degree frame

Fig. 3. Image rendered at 0°

Fig. 4. Image rendered at 90°

From the pair of stereo Figs. 5 and 6 it was possible to reconstruct the dense point cloud presented in the Fig. 7.

Fig. 5. Left image

Fig. 6. Right image

Fig. 7. Reconstructed mesh

As described previously, the detection performed well in different light conditions as we can note in Figs. 8 and 9.

Fig. 8. Test 1

Fig. 9. Test 2

5   Conclusions and Future Work

In this paper, we have proposed an architecture for an automatic system, which provides the necessary scene information for rendering binaural audio. This is the second system of its kind to be documented to date, after the one proposed by S3A spatial audio [2]. Despite the previously presented approach, that reconstructs only from stereo footage, our system has shown the capability to reconstruct from a variety of 360-degree videos. To complement the process, a person detection and tracking method is integrated for associating speech to its source.

For future work, the first task to address is the selection of keyframes in order to reduce the processing needed for the reconstruction. The implementation of our own Structure from Motion system is also considered.

In order to give more robustness to the tracking algorithm, the inference of the inner bounding box must be refined. In addition, a module for plane segmentation must be developed. The final task is the integration of all these modules into one consolidated software, so as to provide binaural audio for storytelling.

Acknowledgments. This article is a result of the project CHIC - Cooperative Holistic view on Internet and Content (project n° 24498), supported by the European Regional Development Fund (ERDF), through the Competitiveness and Internationalization Operational Program (COMPETE 2020) under the PORTUGAL 2020 Partnership Agreement.

References

1. 360-degree projection. https://github.com/bingsyslab/360projection. Accessed 11 June 2018
2. S3A spatial audio. http://www.s3a-spatialaudio.org. Accessed 24 July 2018
3. Akbarzadeh, A., et al.: Towards urban 3D reconstruction from video. In: Proceedings of the Third International Symposium on 3D Data Processing, Visualization, and Transmission (3DPVT 2006). IEEE Computer Society (2006)
4. Andriluka, M., Roth, S., Schiele, B.: People-tracking-by-detection and people-detection-by-tracking. In: 2008 IEEE Conference on Computer Vision and Pattern Recognition, pp. 1–8, June 2008. https://doi.org/10.1109/CVPR.2008.4587583

5. Breuers, S., Beyer, L., Rafi, U., Leibe, B.: Detection-tracking for efficient person analysis: the DetTA pipeline. CoRR abs/1804.10134 (2018). http://arxiv.org/abs/1804.10134
6. Chen, W., Fu, Z., Yang, D., Deng, J.: Single-image depth perception in the wild. CoRR abs/1604.03901 (2016). http://arxiv.org/abs/1604.03901
7. Eigen, D., Puhrsch, C., Fergus, R.: Depth map prediction from a single image using a multi-scale deep network. CoRR abs/1406.2283 (2014). http://arxiv.org/abs/1406.2283
8. Ewerth, R., et al.: Estimating relative depth in single images via rankboost. In: 2017 IEEE International Conference on Multimedia and Expo (ICME), pp. 919–924, July 2017. https://doi.org/10.1109/ICME.2017.8019434
9. Geiger, A., Ziegler, J., Stiller, C.: StereoScan: Dense 3D reconstruction in real-time. In: 2011 IEEE Intelligent Vehicles Symposium (IV), pp. 963–968, June 2011. https://doi.org/10.1109/IVS.2011.5940405
10. Grani, F., et al.: Audio-visual attractors for capturing attention to the screens when walking in cave systems. In: 2014 IEEE VR Workshop: Sonic Interaction in Virtual Environments (SIVE), pp. 3–6, March 2014. https://doi.org/10.1109/SIVE.2014.7006282
11. Güler, R.A., Neverova, N., Kokkinos, I.: DensePose: dense human pose estimation in the wild. CoRR abs/1802.00434 (2018). http://arxiv.org/abs/1802.00434
12. Jafari, O.H., Mitzel, D., Leibe, B.: Real-time RGB-D based people detection and tracking for mobile robots and head-worn cameras. In: 2014 IEEE International Conference on Robotics and Automation (ICRA), pp. 5636–5643, May 2014. https://doi.org/10.1109/ICRA.2014.6907688
13. Kim, A., Eustice, R.M.: Active visual slam for robotic area coverage: theory and experiment. Int. J. Robot. Res. **34**(4–5), 457–475 (2015). https://doi.org/10.1177/0278364914547893
14. Kim, H., Hilton, A.: Block world reconstruction from spherical stereo image pairs. Comput. Vis. Image Underst. **139**, 104–121 (2015). https://doi.org/10.1016/j.cviu.2015.04.001. http://www.sciencedirect.com/science/article/pii/S1077314215000831
15. Kim, H., et al.: Acoustic room modelling using a spherical camera for reverberant spatial audio objects. In: Audio Engineering Society Convention 142, May 2017. http://www.aes.org/e-lib/browse.cfm?elib=18583
16. Lin, T., Goyal, P., Girshick, R.B., He, K., Dollár, P.: Focal loss for dense object detection. CoRR abs/1708.02002 (2017). http://arxiv.org/abs/1708.02002
17. Liu, B., Gould, S., Koller, D.: Single image depth estimation from predicted semantic labels. In: 2010 IEEE Computer Society Conference on Computer Vision and Pattern Recognition, pp. 1253–1260, June 2010. https://doi.org/10.1109/CVPR.2010.5539823
18. Liu, C., Yang, J., Ceylan, D., Yumer, E., Furukawa, Y.: PlaneNet: piece-wise planar reconstruction from a single RGB image. CoRR abs/1804.06278 (2018). http://arxiv.org/abs/1804.06278
19. Polic, M., Förstner, W., Pajdla, T.: Fast and accurate camera covariance computation for large 3D reconstruction (2018)
20. Riazuelo, L., Montano, L., Montiel, J.M.M.: Semantic visual SLAM in populated environments. In: 2017 European Conference on Mobile Robots (ECMR), pp. 1–7, Sept 2017. https://doi.org/10.1109/ECMR.2017.8098697
21. Saurer, O., Pollefeys, M., Hee Lee, G.: Sparse to dense 3D reconstruction from rolling shutter images. In: Proceedings of the IEEE Conference on Computer Vision and Pattern Recognition, pp. 3337–3345 (2016)

22. Spinello, L., Arras, K.O., Triebel, R., Siegwart, R.: A layered approach to people detection in 3D range data. In: Proceedings of the Twenty-Fourth AAAI Conference on Artificial Intelligence, AAAI 2010, pp. 1625–1630. AAAI Press (2010). http://dl.acm.org/citation.cfm?id=2898607.2898866

23. Stewart, R., Andriluka, M., Ng, A.Y.: End-to-end people detection in crowded scenes. In: The IEEE Conference on Computer Vision and Pattern Recognition (CVPR), June 2016

24. Sturm, P., Triggs, B.: A factorization based algorithm for multi-image projective structure and motion. In: Buxton, B., Cipolla, R. (eds.) ECCV 1996. LNCS, vol. 1065, pp. 709–720. Springer, Heidelberg (1996). https://doi.org/10.1007/3-540-61123-1_183

25. Toldo, R., Gherardi, R., Farenzena, M., Fusiello, A.: Hierarchical structure-and-motion recovery from uncalibrated images. Comput. Vis. Image Underst. **140**, 127–143 (2015). https://doi.org/10.1016/j.cviu.2015.05.011. http://www.sciencedirect.com/science/article/pii/S1077314215001228

26. Tome, D., Russell, C., Agapito, L.: Lifting from the deep: convolutional 3D pose estimation from a single image. In: The IEEE Conference on Computer Vision and Pattern Recognition (CVPR), July 2017

27. Wong, K.H., Chang, M.M.Y.: 3D model reconstruction by constrained bundle adjustment. In: 2004 Proceedings of the 17th International Conference on Pattern Recognition, ICPR 2004, vol. 3, pp. 902–905, Aug 2004. https://doi.org/10.1109/ICPR.2004.1334674

28. Yu, R., Russell, C., Campbell, N.D.F., Agapito, L.: Direct, dense, and deformable: Template-based non-rigid 3D reconstruction from RGB video. In: The IEEE International Conference on Computer Vision (ICCV), December 2015

29. Yu, S., Lhuillier, M.: Incremental reconstruction of manifold surface from sparse visual mapping. In: 2012 Second International Conference on 3D Imaging, Modeling, Processing, Visualization Transmission, pp. 293–300, October 2012. https://doi.org/10.1109/3DIMPVT.2012.11

30. Zakharov, A.A., Barinov, A.E.: An algorithm for 3D-object reconstruction from video using stereo correspondences. Pattern Recogn. Image Anal. **25**(1), 117–121 (2015). https://doi.org/10.1134/S1054661815010228

31. Zhang, G., Liu, J., Li, H., Chen, Y.Q., Davis, L.S.: Joint human detection and head pose estimation via multistream networks for RGB-D videos. IEEE Signal Process. Lett. **24**(11), 1666–1670 (2017). https://doi.org/10.1109/LSP.2017.2731952

32. Zhou, H., Zou, D., Pei, L., Ying, R., Liu, P., Yu, W.: StructSLAM: visual SLAM with building structure lines. IEEE Trans. Veh. Technol. **64**(4), 1364–1375 (2015). https://doi.org/10.1109/TVT.2015.2388780

33. Zhuo, W., Salzmann, M., He, X., Liu, M.: Indoor scene structure analysis for single image depth estimation. In: 2015 IEEE Conference on Computer Vision and Pattern Recognition (CVPR), pp. 614–622, June 2015. https://doi.org/10.1109/CVPR.2015.7298660

User Behaviour Analysis and Personalized TV Content Recommendation

Ana Carolina Ribeiro[1]([⊠]) [iD], Rui Frazão[2], and Jorge Oliveira e Sá[1] [iD]

[1] University of Minho, Guimarães, Portugal
anacfrl@hotmail.com, jos@dsi.uminho.pt
[2] University of Aveiro, Aveiro, Portugal
ruifilipefrazao@ua.pt

Abstract. Nowadays, there are many channels and television (TV) programs available, and when the viewer is confronted with this amount of information has difficulty in deciding which wants to see. However, there are moments of the day that viewers see always the same channels or programs, that is, viewers have TV content consumption habits. The aim of this paper was to develop a recommendation system that to be able to recommend TV content considering the viewer profile, time and weekday.

For the development of this paper, were used Design Science Research (DSR) and Cross Industry Standard Process for Data Mining (CRISP-DM) methodologies. For the development of the recommendation model, two approaches were considered: a deterministic approach and a Machine Learning (ML) approach. In the ML approach, K-means algorithm was used to be possible to combine STBs with similar profiles. In the deterministic approach the behaviors of the viewers are adjusted to a profile that will allow you to identify the content you prefer. Here, recommendation system analyses viewer preferences by hour and weekday, allowing customization of the system, considering your historic, recommending what he wants to see at certain time and weekday.

ML approach was not used due to amount of data extracted and computational resources available. However, through deterministic methods it was possible to develop a TV content recommendation model considering the viewer profile, the weekday and the hour. Thus, with the results it was possible to understand which viewer profiles where the ML can be used.

Keywords: Recommender systems · Machine learning ·
User behaviour analytics

1 Introduction

Currently, consumers have access to a massive quantity of information about lots of products everyday, which makes the decision-making of choosing to process harder. This problem is known in technical literature as "Information Overload", which refers to the fact that there are finite limits to the ability of humans to assimilate and process information [1]. This is considered a major difficulty in decision-making process in many fields.

© ICST Institute for Computer Sciences, Social Informatics and Telecommunications Engineering 2019
Published by Springer Nature Switzerland AG 2019. All Rights Reserved
P. Cortez et al. (Eds.): INTETAIN 2018, LNICST 273, pp. 127–136, 2019.
https://doi.org/10.1007/978-3-030-16447-8_13

Specifically, in television (TV) consumption, growing number of channels available leads to a more complex and time-consuming choice of content to the viewer. In this paper, the user behind the screen is called 'viewer'. With the increase of channels, zapping and TV programming magazines are not effective in the selection of content [2].

Thus, the objective of this paper is to develop a model capable of describing and inferring the preferences of TV content of viewers for a selection more personalized, based on the records activity of Set Top Boxes (STBs). STBs do not present user profiles, which means that if there is more than one viewer using STB, it is not possible to differentiate. To overcome this situation, it was decided to analyse each activity record of STB per hour.

This paper aims to develop a model that can describe a viewer in each time-slot by using information from the preferences profile. The viewer behaviour will be analysed to be adjusted to a behaviour profile that will allow to quickly identify the type of content he is looking for.

In this way, the goal of this paper is the construction of a prototype that, for each STB and in each time-slot, choose one of the three types of solutions:

1. When time-slots do not have enough visualizations to infer who is viewing, does not perform a recommendation.
2. When the time-slot history shows a regular pattern of visualizations, this allows to make a prediction of TV content with a very high probability of being accepted by the viewer.
3. When the time-slots history shows a complex pattern of visualizations, in these situations, there is a high probability that the Machine Learning (ML) techniques will work.

For the recommendation system development, two approaches are considered: a deterministic approach and ML based approach with K-Means algorithm.

The Design Science Research (DSR) methodology enables the creation and evaluation of information technology artefacts to solve organizational problems and involves a rigorous process of developing artefacts to solve the identified problems, contributing to the research and evaluating the projects [3]. This paper aims to create an artefact based on deterministic or ML approaches for an effective recommendation of TV contents to viewers. Thus, this paper takes in to account the guidelines of the DSR in parallel with the data mining methodology CRISP-DM [3].

This paper is organized as: Sect. 2 describes the related work; in Sect. 3 the data available, the most important features and the data statistical analysis performed is presented; Sect. 4 describes the recommendation model development and ML technologies used; Sect. 5 presents the results obtained from the recommendation model developed and the evaluation of the results. Finally, the conclusions and future work of this paper are summarized in Sect. 6.

2   Related Work

2.1   Recommender Systems

Since the world is becoming more and more digital, it is considered the existence of a parallel between humans and technology: on the one hand, individuals use more and more technology, and on the other, digital systems have become more and more centred on the user. This way, the systems should allow users to be able to synthesize information and explore the data [4].

Therefore, there is a need for computing techniques that facilitate this research and the extraction of information in the interest of the user. One of the solutions to this problem is the use of ML techniques to find explicit and implicit patterns of user preferences, for the purpose of customizing the search for content of the user's interest [1].

An approach used to the suggestion of the content of the user's interest is the recommendation systems [5]. A recommendation system can be defined as any system that provides the user with recommendations of services, products or certain potentially interesting content. To provide suggestions and help users in decision-making, the recommendation systems should be include some characteristics such as users' needs, their difficulties, goals, preferences and some know-how about domain of business [4, 5]. They consist on the capability of providing suggestions for items[1] [5].

There are several recommender systems, but the most used are content-based recommender systems, collaborative and hybrid systems [1]:

Content-based Systems – systems that try to recommend new items that are like items that a user has shown interest in the past.

Collaborative Filtering systems – the recommendations are based on the analysis of the similarity between users. The suggested items are those that users with similar preferences have had an interest in the past.

Hybrid systems – systems that implement a combination of two or more recommendation techniques. These systems try to take advantage of all techniques used to improve the performance of the system and reduce the disadvantages of each technique used individually.

The interest in the recommender systems is increasingly high, due to the growing demand in applications capable of providing personalized recommendations and dealing with information overload [5]. Some challenges and limitations can be found in the recommendation systems, namely:

Cold-start - There are some situations in which the lack of data causes the recommender system not to make recommendations or the recommendations generated do not present a high level of confidence [6]. For example, in content-based filtering, it is necessary for the system to have access to the user's interests in the past, to decide which items are like those. This problem may occur because of the addition of new users or a new item [6].

---

[1] "Item" is the general term used to denote what the system recommends to users. Products, movies, music and news are some examples of what can be recommended.

Data dispersion - Data dispersal is a common problem in most recommender systems since users typically classify only a small proportion of the items available [5].

Limited context - The location, time, date, etc., are some of the context factors that recommender systems should take into consideration. In addition, factors such as user emotion, mood and other parameters should also be considered as they influence users' decisions [5].

2.2   TV Centred Recommender Systems

With the rise of TV content and new functionalities available it was necessary to find adequate tools to help users to choose the content of their interest. Although recommender systems allow users to take an active role and request content on the fly, it also gives the possibility to recommend personalized content based on the users preferences without a prior request [7]. Interactive platforms like Electronic Programming Guide emerged as a tool to help TV consumption. On Video on Demand (VOD) recommender systems emerge as a proposal to improve the process of discovery of new movies, with a relative success and that makes recommender systems have a high importance in the field of TV. These systems tend to have a more effective impact on platforms of Subscription VOD (SVOD), an example of that is Netflix [8].

The development of effective recommendation systems is complex due to some particularities of the TV content. One of the difficulties of systems that have access to a catch-up TV system is that they are constantly entering new content for the catalogue and the older contents are removed due to the time window of the automatic recordings to be limited [8].

An important factor in TV recommender systems is time. For example, a viewer's favourite movie can be displayed in a channel while the viewer is watching another program with less interest, so this is the right time to suggest the movie to the viewer if the recommender systems not suggest the movie to the viewer at right time, this recommender system becomes an imprecise recommender system with high cost to maintain and users tend to disable this kind of functionality [9].

3   Data Analysis

The life cycle of CRISP-DM methodology consists of 6 phases: business understanding, data understanding, data preparation, modelling, evaluation and implementation and the sequence of the phases is not rigid [10].

In the data understanding phase of CRISP-DM, it was found that data by the STBs correspond to 5 months of registers (from January to May) of 2017 of a total of 1.5 million STBs. For this paper, data were provided by a telecommunications organization in Portugal. The data provided presents different types of information about TV contents. To complete the data understanding phase, some data statistical exploration was performed to find out mistakes, missing values and to know the attributes meanings. Initially, the data distributions were analysed to know the normal patterns from population analysed so that, when extracting samples for experimentation, it was possible to evaluate if these would be representative of the remaining population or not. Some examples are given below.

It was calculated the distribution of viewing time in hours and per day, for all STBs between January and March. With this distribution, it was possible to observe that there are regularly higher values corresponding to weekend values, that is, viewers see more TV at the weekend. This result corresponds with reality because, in general, people have more free time on the weekend. An analysis was also performed about the content viewing time, because the number of view records may be high, but the duration time of each record can be very small. In this way, the viewing time of television content is a relevant factor in understanding viewer preferences. From this analysis, it was found that 38% of the records have a viewing percentage of 75%–100%, which means they see a large part of the content or in your totality. These results contrast with the 35% of records that have a viewing percentage between 0–15%, which means that they only see part of the content and where zapping moments can be represented. There is a class that represents views above 100% (views with a time greater than the total time of the program). This phenomenon can occur if the viewer pauses the program for a long period or uses de timeshift functionality and reviews parts of the program. These are just a few examples.

It was also carried out, in the data quality, some inconsistencies were found, such as, missing values and errors (for example, the same program is classified as a series and a program, simultaneously). The identified errors and missing values were reported, and others are corrected.

In consideration of dimensionality of the data, in the data selection phase it was decided to use a sample with only 3 months of 500 STBs that correspond to about 1 million of views. It was decided to select only 500 STBs because the available computational resources were not enough to support the total amount of data and due to the limited time for prototype development. In addition, of the total of 5 months, only 3 (March, April and May) were selected due to the constraints of the available computational resources. Thus, it was decided to exclude January for having only 15 days of records and February for being the shortest in relation to the remainder. Thus, it will be possible to use two months as training and a month of testing. Still in the selection phase of the data were selected some attributes that were considered relevant to the development of the recommendation system, for example: programs, channels, channel thematic, time and weekday of visualization.

Thus, after the phases of understanding and preparing data it is possible to apply modelling techniques to the dataset in the modelling phase, described in the next section.

4 Recommendation Model

4.1 Technologies

Among the numerous ML technologies available, chosen for the development of this project was H2O.ai along with Python programming language. H2O.ai is a Java-based open source, in-memory, distributed, fast, and scalable ML and predictive analytics platform that allows to build ML models on big data [11]. H2O.ai was recently classified as a leader technology in Gartner's Magic Quadrant for Data Science & ML Platforms [12]. H2O.ai also lacks methods for data manipulation and data visualization compared to the most used python packages for data handling, Pandas, and data visualization, Matplotlib.

In addition to the H2O.ai, two notebooks were used for project development: Apache Zeppelin and Jupyter. Zeppelin is an open-source notebook that allows the ingestion, exploration and data visualization. Zeppelin allows data visualization in various formats allowing the user to get a quick and easy data perception [13]. Jupyter notebook, such as Zeppelin, it is an open-source notebook that allows you to create and share documents with code, visualizations, and narrative text. This notebook provides a suitable web-based application to capture the entire computing process: development, documentation and code execution [14].

Zeppelin was used for the data understanding phase due to the quality it presents in the data visualization. In data processing phase and recommendation system development, Jupyter was favourite by the ability to be used in tasks requiring greater code development as transformation of Data, statistical modelling or machine learning.

4.2 Recommendation Model Development

In the model development (modelling phase in CRISP-DM), as previously mentioned, two approaches were tested: a deterministic approach and a ML approach.

In the ML approach, a clustering experience was performed with the aim of finding similar visualization profiles through STBs visualization and consequently recommendations are based on the similarities found. For this experience, where the goal is to find data similarities and to group them with these similarities, would be necessary an unsupervised learning algorithm, since data are not previously classified. Given these requirements, the algorithm chosen to apply in modelling phase was the K-means.

In the deterministic approach, viewers behaviors will be analysed to be adjusted to a profile that will allow you to identify the type of content looking for, considering the 3 types of actuation identified in the introduction. Initially, the following profiles were identified:

- **No previews** - STBs do not present visualizations records and, therefore, recommendation is not carried out;
- **Program preference** - STBs present an explicit program preference if the percentage of the content display is equal to or greater than a parameter X, in this case, 70%. In this case, the most viewed program is recommended;
- **Channel preference** - STBs present an explicit channel preference if the percentage of the channel display is equal to or greater than a parameter, in this case 70%. So, the most viewed channel is recommended;
- **No pattern** - STBs present a complex visualizations pattern, without preferences defined.

Still in this approach, after a new problem analyse, it was decided to reformulate the model to increase the capacity of solution (Fig. 1). In this new analysis, in addition to the profiles of program preferences and channel preferences, new profiles arose where the recommendation goes through a set of 3 suggestions of the most viewed programs or channels, that is, in which the sum of the percentages of visualizations is equal or more than a new parameter Y and, in this case, Y = 90%. In addition to the previously found profiles, the following have emerged:

- **Top 3 programs** – recommendation of the 3 most viewed programs (sum of the duration of visualizations of the 3 programs must be Y = 90%);
- **Top 3 channels** – recommendation of the 3 most viewed channels (sum of the duration of the visualizations of the 3 programs must be Y = 90%);
- **Thematic preference** – recommendation of the channel thematic most viewed;
- **No pattern** – no default preference set.

The 'No pattern' profile represents the profiles with an undefined visualizations pattern and recommendation by deterministic methods would not be appropriate. Here, the way of recommending would pass through ML techniques if it was justified to employ machines in this processing, that is, if the percentage of STBs in this profile is significant.

After analysing of these two approaches, Sect. 6 will be presented the results of the two approaches and the justification for which a deterministic approach has been used.

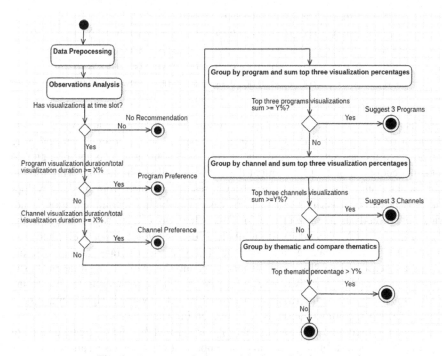

Fig. 1. Recommendation model: deterministic approach.

5   Result Analysis and Evaluation

In ML approach, the K-means algorithm was trained with records of March and April, for a weekday and time. In Table 1, it is possible to observe some observations that have been grouped because they are similar. The values from 1 to 13 of the Table 1 columns, correspond to the channel thematics. The purpose of this approach is to group the STBs with similar profiles (in this case, considering the channel thematic) on a given day at a certain time. In Table 1, it is possible to verify that, all STBs have a significant visualization percentage of thematic 5, which corresponds to the thematic 'Information'. This means that this set of STBs, on a certain day at a certain time, see the same thematic and, therefore, have been grouped. However, a cost-benefit assessment of the application of this approach was realized, and it was rejected because, given the amount of data and resources available, it would not be possible in the time available for the realization of the project.

Table 1. Cluster observations.

Thematic	STB									
	1	2	3	4	**5**	6	7	8	9	10
1	0.02	0.35	0.00	0.00	**0.61**	0.00	0.00	0.00	0.00	0.00
12	0.00	0.00	0.00	0.00	**0.69**	0.00	0.00	0.30	0.00	0.00
96	0.00	0.00	0.00	0.00	**0.86**	0.00	0.00	0.00	0.00	0.13
130	0.00	0.29	0.00	0.00	**0.70**	0.00	0.00	0.00	0.00	0.00
131	0.00	0.00	0.00	0.00	**0.48**	0.42	0.00	0.00	0.00	0.07

In this way, the model was developed through the deterministic approach. For the application of this model, March and April correspond to the training set and May corresponds to the test set for a sampling of 100 SBTs. The goal is to get through two months of records to predict the content that viewers will see in the following month.

In Tables 2 and 3 it is possible to observe results obtained from model development. It is possible to verify percentage of cases in which a recommendation is not carried out correctly is 32.68% (Table 3). This value may change with changes in the values of the X and Y parameters of the model (70% and 90%, respectively) and may achieve lower values, making the recommendation more accurate. In Table 3, the percentage of cases where the recommendation cannot be made through deterministic methods correspond to the 'No pattern' profile, that is, corresponds to 7% of the 32.68%. It is necessary, in the future, to assess whether this value is significant. If so, a machine learning recommendation system may be implemented.

About correct recommendations (Table 2), it is verified that the percentage value of the profile 'No visualization' is high. This is an important value because it allows to know which time-slots where it is not necessary to employ resources financial and computational resources to carry out recommendations. Also, 'program Preference' profile and 'Top 3 Program' profile present a percentage of correct recommendations lower than the percentage of incorrect recommendations. This is because it was not possible to use meta-information on the programs of the period studied in the model development.

Thus, about 67% of the recommendations made by the deterministic model are correct.

Table 2. Correct recommendations

Class	Occur.	Proportions
No visualization	7383	43.95%
Program preference	701	4.17%
Channel preference	908	5.40%
Top 3 programs	762	4.54%
Top 3 channels	1179	7.02%
Thematic preference	377	2.24%
Total		67.32%

Table 3. Incorrect recommendations

Class	Occur.	Proportions
Program preference	1564	9.31%
Channel preference	569	3.39%
Top 3 programs	1519	9.04%
Top 3 channels	544	3.24%
Thematic preference	81	0.48%
No pattern	1213	7.22%
Total		32.68%

6 Conclusion and Future Work

With the development of this recommendation model, it is noticeable that with only statistical and deterministic methods is possible to make recommendations based on visualization history, making the model less computationally expensive and faster. Even though the parameters have not been optimized, the results seem to fit the expectations for a recommender system on this kind of system. Like most recommender systems, this model needs data to retrieve information about users' preferences and without it a user is not capable of receiving recommendations.

There are some improvements that could be made to improve the recommendation accuracy like standardizing the program titles on the source data, analysing the threshold values used in the model (X and Y parameters) and tune them to achieve better results and reduce the percentage of the "No Pattern" class.

In a next step of this project, an evaluation of the significance of the values of the "No Pattern" class could be made based on the cost-benefit ratio of that operation. Making recommendations to that set of users could be computationally expensive and not financially worth.

Acknowledgement. This work has been supported by COMPETE: POCI-01-0145-FEDER-007043 and FCT (Fundação para a Ciência e Tecnologia) within the Project Scope: UID/CEC/00319/2013 and was developed in partnership with AlticeLabs.

References

1. Cotter, P., Smyth, B.: PTV: intelligent personalised TV guides. In: Proceedings of the Seventeenth National Conference on Artificial Intelligence and Twelfth Conference on Innovative Applications of Artificial Intelligence, pp. 957–964 (2000)
2. Soares, M., Viana, P.: TV recommendation and personalization systems: integrating broadcast and video on-demand services. Adv. Electr. Comput. Eng. **14**(1), 115–120 (2014)

3. Peffers, K., Tuunanen, T., Rothenberger, M., Chatterjee, S.: A design science research methodology for information systems research. J. Manag. Inf. Syst. **24**(3), 45–78 (2007)
4. Negre, E.: Information and Recommender Systems. Wiley, Hoboken (2015)
5. Francesco, R., Lior, R., Shapira, B.: Recommender System Handbook, 1st edn. Springer, US (2011). https://doi.org/10.1007/978-0-387-85820-3
6. Madadipouya, K., Chelliah, S.: A literature review on recommender systems algorithms, techniques and evaluations. BRAIN Broad Res. Artif. Intell. Neurosci. **8**(2), 109–124 (2017)
7. Blanco-Fernández, Y., Pazos-Arias, J.J., Gil-Solla, A., Ramos-Cabrer, M., Lopez-Nores, M., Barragans-Martinez, B.: AVATAR : a multi-agent TV recommender system using MHP applications. In: IEEE International Conference on e-Technology, e-Commerce and e-Service, pp. 660–665 (2005)
8. Abreu, J., Nogueira, J., Becker, V., Cardoso, B.: Survey of catch-up TV and other time-shift services: a comprehensive analysis and taxonomy of linear and nonlinear television. In: Telecommunication Systems, 1st ed., pp. 57–74 (2017)
9. Oh, J., Kim, S., Kim, J., Yu, H.: When to recommend: a new issue on TV show recommendation. Inf. Sci. (Ny) **280**(1), 261–274 (2014)
10. Chapman, P., et al.: Crisp-DM 1.0. Cris. Consort. 76 (2000)
11. H2O.ai: Welcome to H2O 3 — H2O 3.20.0.3 documentation. Welcome to H2O 3 (2018). http://docs.h2o.ai/h2o/latest-stable/h2o-docs/welcome.html. Accessed 01 July 2018
12. Idoine, C.J., Krensky, P., Brethenoux, E., Hare, J., Sicular, S., Vashisth, S.: Magic quadrant for data science and machine-learning platforms, no. February, pp. 1–26 (2018)
13. Zeppelin, A.: Apache Zeppelin 0.8.0 documentation. What is Apache Zeppelin? (2018). https://zeppelin.apache.org/docs/0.8.0/. Accessed 01 July 2018
14. Jupyter: The Jupyter notebook — Jupyter notebook 5.5.0 documentation (2015). https://jupyter-notebook.readthedocs.io/en/stable/. Accessed 01 July 2018

Virtual and Augmented Reality Interfaces in Shared Game Environments: A Novel Approach

Francesco De Pace$^{(\boxtimes)}$, Federico Manuri, Andrea Sanna, and Davide Zappia

Dipartimento di Automatica e Informatica, Politecnico di Torino, Corso Duca degli Abruzzi 24, 10129 Torino, Italy
`francesco.depace@polito.it`

Abstract. Augmented Reality (AR) and Virtual Reality (VR) have been usu-ally addressed as two separated worlds and recent studies try to address the problem of merging the AR and VR applications into a single "environment", providing a system that relies on both paradigms. The constant release of new hardware interfaces for both wearable AR and Immersive VR opens up new possibilities for the gaming area and many others. However, even if there are researches that explore the usage of AR and VR in the same application, videogames are deployed for one environment or the other depending on their strengths and flaws and the type of experience they can offer to the player, in order to exalt the peculiarities of the chosen medium. A novel approach would be to provide a multiplayer system that enables the users to play the same (or similar) experience through either an AR or VR interface: the player could freely choose the interface, based on several factors such as hardware availability, environment, physical limitations or personal preferences. In this paper, a pre-liminary study on a multiplayer game system for both AR and VR interfaces is proposed. A chess game experience is provided and a comparison through a System Usability Scale (SUS) questionnaire allowed to establish if both inter-faces provided a satisfactory game experience and to highlight both hardware limitations and further interface enhancements.

Keywords: Augmented reality · Virtual reality · Shared environment

1 Introduction

Since its definition in 1994 by Milgram and Kishino [1], the term Mixed Reality (MR) has been used to denote all the technologies adopted to merge the real world with virtually generated contents. Depending on the content which is more relevant in the Mixed Reality experience, it is possible to further distinguish between Augmented Reality (AR), used to define any case in which the real world is enhanced through virtual objects, and Augmented Virtuality (AV), used to describe a virtual world enriched with real video elements.

Overall, Mixed Reality and Virtual Reality (VR) are characterized by the presence (or absence) of the real world: for this reason, different types of interaction paradigms

© ICST Institute for Computer Sciences, Social Informatics and Telecommunications Engineering 2019
Published by Springer Nature Switzerland AG 2019. All Rights Reserved
P. Cortez et al. (Eds.): INTETAIN 2018, LNICST 273, pp. 137–147, 2019.
https://doi.org/10.1007/978-3-030-16447-8_14

are adopted when deploying an application for one of these two technologies. Since Virtual Reality relies only on computer generated contents, the game experience and the interface aim at casting off the user into a fictional reality, detached from the real world. On the other hand, since Mixed Reality (and especially AR) environments are based on real world elements, the game experience is determined by the interaction of the player with the real world, whereas the virtual elements have the purpose of guiding the user and providing a feedback to its actions.

Among the diverse fields of use for both AR and VR, the entertainment industry has always covered a main role in the progress and improvements of these two technologies, due to the significative income of this industry [2] and the desire of videogame players to be part of the game [3]. AR and VR have numerous applications in the entertainment area [4–7] and most importantly they can be applied to create videogames [8–12].

Till now, AR and VR have been usually addressed as two separated worlds: videogames are deployed for one environment or the other depending on their strengths and flaws and the type of experience they can offer to the player, in order to exalt the peculiarities of the chosen medium. Even if the two interfaces are merged together into a single application, till now only two options are adopted: they are either used subsequently in a single player application to provide different kinds of interaction, or they provide different kinds of interaction to different users in a multiplayer environment.

In this paper, a preliminary study on a multiplayer game system for both AR and VR interfaces is proposed. The system enables the player to play the same game both with an AR, wearable device (the Microsoft Hololens) and an immersive, VR one (the Oculus Rift). A chess game experience is provided for both devices since the environment is not relevant to the game mechanics but only to the interaction model. A comparison between the two devices through a System Usability Scale (SUS) questionnaire allowed to establish if both the AR and VR interfaces provided a satisfactory game experience and to highlight both hardware limitations and further interface enhancements.

The paper is organized as follows: Sect. 2 briefly explores the state of the art of AR and VR for gaming. Section 3 analyzes what an ideal AR-VR framework should look like whereas in Sect. 4 our solution is described. In Sect. 5 the tests performed to compare the user interfaces are presented together with the results analysis. Finally, Sect. 6 provides the conclusion and possible future works.

2 State of the Art

First examples of commercial VR headsets for gaming can be dated back to the early nineties, such as the Nintendo Virtual Boy and the Virtual I-O iGlasses. Due to the huge improvements in computer graphic cards started in the second half of the nineties, the VR market was abandoned in favor of traditional videogames till 2010, when new, technological compelling hardware solutions for VR were released, such as the Oculus Rift, and later the HTC Vive. Until the mid-noughties, the technological progress kept AR as a domain for researchers, since costly, ad-hoc hardware was necessary for playing AR games. The release of smartphones, tablets and other wearable devices allowed everyone to possess an AR enabled hardware; at the same time, scientific researches on AR during the noughties explored and investigated computer graphic algorithms for AR, leading to the concept of AR frameworks and toolkits, such as the ARToolKit[1] and the Metaio SDK[2]. Thus, with both hardware and software solutions for AR, the entertainment industry started investing in such technology.

First researches on AR for gaming can be dated back to the late nineties [13, 14]. Human Pacman, presented by Cheok et al. in 2004, is probably the first attempt at merging AR and VR in the same experience [15]. In this outdoor game, one player embodies Pacman in his/her efforts to collect all the coins available through the level, whereas the other players represent the ghosts that try to stop Pacman. With all these players interacting through an AR, wearable interface, Pacman can rely on an external helper represented by a player that can watch and monitor the position of all the AR players through a VR interface. Epidemic Menace is another example of multiplayer system with players cooperating with both AR and VR interfaces, whereas the game mechanics, perspectives and interaction with other users change depending on the chosen interface [16].

Other recent studies try to address the problem of merging the AR and VR applications into a single environment, providing a system that relies on both paradigms. However, the proposed results can be classified in two categories: the first one comprehends all the applications that embody the Augmented Virtuality paradigm; these applications are usually experienced through Immersive Virtual Reality hardware. Clash Tanks is an example of this category, since the player is immersed in a virtual reality cockpit with a virtual monitor displaying real word camera input of a physical robot, enhanced through AR chassis' decorations [17]. The second category comprehends applications whose interfaces change between virtual and augmented reality depending on the game flow; these applications are usually base on handheld, mobile devices such as smartphones and tablets. Example of this approach are the driving safety game proposed by Vera et al. [18] and the Eduventure game proposed by Ferdinand et al. [19]. Overall, even if there are researches that explore the usage of AR and VR in the same application, a system which allows the users to play the same game with both an AR or a VR interface has not been investigated yet.

3 Shared Reality Environment Analysis

Linking the AR and the VR worlds, as if they are two overlapped realities, means to represent the same things seen from different point of views, generating new unexplored forms of interaction. Setting up a conjunction between an AR world and a VR one concerns at least three different issues: the creation of a proper connection; the development of different AR and VR interfaces; the analysis of the frame of reference.

A multiplayer-cooperative system requires the development of a reliable communication protocol. Since the AR player can freely move around in the real environment,

---

[1] ARToolKit, https://www.hitl.washington.edu/artoolkit/.

[2] Metaio, https://en.wikipedia.org/wiki/Metaio.

a wireless system is expected. Moreover, players can be delocalized in different zones of the world, thus short-distance communication protocols, such as Bluetooth, are not suitable and a connection passing through the Internet is necessary. The most known communication typologies are client-server and point to point. The choice of the protocol type strongly depends on the type of shared environment that has to be realized.

Interfaces represent one of the most critical aspects of an interaction system. In a shared reality environment different users that belong to either AR o VR should be able to interact using the interface that most suit their specific environment. The AR interface should offer a proper interaction with both the real world and the virtual one to establish a synergy between them. On the other hand, the VR interface has to allow the user to properly interact with the virtual world; the main difference with respect to the AR interface lies in that the VR user acts and moves in the real environment but his/her interactions occur only in the virtual environment. Moreover, since a shared reality environment is based on an interaction among two or more users, these interfaces have to exchange data in real time to ensure an efficient use of the system.

In a shared reality scenario, at least two different frames of reference exist: the system of reference of the AR user and the one of the VR user. While in the VR system the player is just placed in a global reference system, the AR system results to be slightly more complex. In order to augment the real world, data relative to position, orientation and scale of a target should be extracted. Once the system has acquired them, it is possible to generate at least two distinct systems of reference, called *target centered mode* and *camera centered mode*. In the first approach, when the target has been tracked, the target itself is placed in the origin of the global reference system and the player position is relative to the target. On the other hand, in the camera center mode, the player is placed in the origin and the target position is user-related.

To establish a link between the AR and VR system of references, it is possible to realize two different systems: absolute system of reference or distinct systems of reference. In the first system, only one frame of reference exists and therefore a reliable connection must be established to synchronize all the 3D models among the players (for instance, a client-server architecture). In the second configuration, the AR frame and the VR one are separated and the transformations are applied independently of the virtual assets in each reference frame. Only transformation's data are exchanged, thus a client-server architecture results to be redundant and a point to point connection could be preferred.

4 The Proposed System

It is unusual to think about an application, and more specifically a videogame, that is designed independently from the environment: even if the context or theme could be shared among virtual and augmented reality games, the game experience is mostly different. It seemed relevant to select a tabletop game for our research instead of a videogame for several reasons. Firstly, deciding otherwise would mean to select a game designed either for virtual reality and then to port it to augmented reality or the opposite: however, this choice would probably advantage the original experience versus the port; in some cases, it could even be impossible to provide the same experience for both environments. Secondly, the most famous tabletop games have been ported into virtual reality environment, such as Monopoly, Scrabble or Risk. Among them, chess seemed the most appropriate as a use case for multiple reasons: it is well known world-wide, it has already been used to research AR game interfaces (e.g. [20, 21]) and it offers a strategic deepness that could allow to evaluate if and how the interface affects the game experience, whereas this could be less feasible with a more simplistic game. Lastly, since the developing of AR/VR videogames is still not widespread, it is not possible to find adequate references or guidelines to develop them from scratch. Thus, a well- known tabletop game consists indeed in a legitimate choice.

The aim is to compare two different interfaces in a chess shared gaming environment. Specifically, this shared scenario is composed by two users that can play using an AR device and a VR one. The VR user can interact with a virtual chessboard using an immersive virtual device, whereas the AR user plays with a real chessboard composed by real and virtual pieces, using an AR wearable device. It consists of a multi-user system: different players, using distinct interfaces, can exchange data interactively. In the subsequent paragraph, the configuration of this project is presented.

4.1 System Architecture

In a chess game, only the start and the end positions of the piece that it is going to be moved by one of the players have to be exchanged, thus the proposed system is composed by two different reference's systems that exchange data in real time on a socket connection. The transformations relative to the 3D assets (movement and rotations of the game piece) are applied locally in each system of reference. The proposed use case consists of two devices connected on the same LAN: an Oculus Rift DK2 Kit has been used for playing in the VR environment and the Microsoft Hololens[3] glasses have been used for the AR scenario. Since the AR user plays with the real chess board, an image target has been employed to correctly align the virtual assets on the game grid. The software architecture has been realized using Unity3D as IDE. In addition, the AR application has been developed using three external libraries: the MixedRealityToolkit-Unity[4] for managing the interaction, the Vuforia library[5] for the target detection and the LiteNetLib[6] library for the socket communication. The VR application has been developed using the SteamVR Plugin[7] to get access to the Oculus Rift DK2 hardware.

---

[3] https://www.microsoft.com/it-it/hololens.

[4] https://github.com/Microsoft/MixedRealityToolkit-Unity.

[5] https://developer.vuforia.com/downloads/sdk.

[6] https://github.com/RevenantX/LiteNetLib.

[7] https://assetstore.unity.com/packages/templates/systems/steamvr-plugin-32647.

4.2 Game Play

The VR user visualizes and interacts with the 3D assets. Specifically, with a virtual chessboard and the virtual chess pieces. Differently, the AR user interacts with his real pieces against the virtual representation of the enemy pieces.

The AR user is the white player while the VR user is the black one. At the beginning of the game, the AR player moves, changing the position of the real white piece. At the same time, the virtual representation of the corresponding white piece is moved on the VR application, thus the two environments remain aligned. When the VR user plays moving a black virtual piece, the corresponding 3D piece is moved in the AR application on the real chessboard.

4.3 Interfaces

Since users play the same game using two different systems of interaction and visualization, two different interfaces have been developed. Nevertheless, the sequence of interactions is identical for both the environments (VR and AR) and it is represented by the following work-flow: piece selection and piece movement.

VR Interface. The Oculus DK2 does not provide any form on interaction, thus an XBOX 360 joystick has been added to properly interact with the game. Several on-line chess games[8,9] allow the user to select and move the desired piece without occluding the remain pieces. In addition, when the piece has been selected, the available moves are highlighted on the chess board. In order to achieve this behavior, it is possible to utilize the user's gaze to interact with the chess board. Firstly, a ray-cast is performed, starting from the center of the virtual camera. Then, when the ray-cast hits a tile of the virtual chess board, the tile is highlighted in yellow and a small 3D cube (called cursor) is rendered at the hit coordinates. To select a piece, the user has to look to the tile containing a movable piece, highlighting it, then he/she can select it using the "A button" on the joystick. Then, the available moves for the selected piece are shown on the chessboard, highlighting the corresponding tiles. If one or more of the available moves intersect an enemy piece, that specific tile is highlighted in red. The user can then select the final tile and the corresponding piece is moved when the "A button" is pressed.

Since in the AR experience the player could freely move around the real environment to change his/her view point, the same feature was added through the software to the VR interface: the user can freely rotate the chessboard around the global y and x axes to analyze the game field from other perspectives. Moreover, since several chess games offer either a single top view to visualize the entire game board or a 45° view, both have been made available to the user through shortcuts.

AR Interface. The AR interface is composed by three different layers: gaze layer, gesture layer, and sound layer. The gaze layer manages the interaction with the tiles of the chessboard. Although the main functioning is the same as the gaze of the VR

---

[8] https://www.chess.com/.

[9] http://www.chesscube.com/.

interface, there are some differences. Firstly, the AR user is interacting with the real chessboard, thus it has been necessary to instantiate a virtual chessboard aligned with the real one but invisible to the user. In this way, when the ray cast hits the virtual hidden chessboard, a 3D cursor is rendered on the real chess board and the corresponding virtual tile is highlighted, correctly aligned with the real one. In order to establish a connection between the real piece and its virtual representation, a mechanism to synchronize the real move and the virtual one must be pursued. The Hololens glasses is capable of recognizing two gestures, the air tap and the bloom gesture. Taking advantage of this capability, a connection between the real piece and the virtual one can be established: firstly, when a tile containing a real movable piece is highlighted, it can be selected using the air tap gesture and the available moves are shown on the real chess board. If one or more of the available moves intersect an enemy piece, that specific tile is highlighted in red. Then, the VR interface receives the data regarding the piece that is going to be moved. Afterwards, the AR user, moving the 3D cursor on an available tile, can select it performing another time the air tap gesture. Finally, the VR interface receives the data regarding the final position and the virtual piece is moved in the VR application.

Fig. 1. In both environments, when the player has to move the piece, the available moves are shown on the game field. (Color figure online)

To complete the synchronization, the AR user has to physically move the real piece on the tile selected during the procedure described above. In order to ease this action, a pre-recorded voice informs the user to move the real piece. Moreover, the user can activate or deactivate a virtual green grid overlapped on the real chessboard to better understand the position of the virtual pieces. To exploit the virtual models and to improve the entertainment of the players, animations have been used to represent the attack and the "death" of the virtual 3D pieces. Animations have been widely used to enhance the game experience, they can convey emotions, motivations and intentions to viewers [22]. Finally, a side user interface is provided in both environments to inform the user about the identity of the current player. Figure 1 shows the AR and the VR interfaces.

5   Tests and Results Analysis

In order to compare the usability of the AR and VR interfaces, some tests have been held at the Politecnico di Torino. Users were either master-degree students, Ph.D. student or research assistant of the Computer Science Department. Twenty volunteers took part in the test, 12 men and 8 women, with ages that ranged between 21 and 34 years. Testers have been divided into 10 pairs, and each player tested both interfaces. A questionnaire has been created and proposed to the users, using the System Usability Scale (SUS) [23] ranked with a five *Likert scale*. The questionnaire was divided into three different sections: the first one was about user's information, whereas the second and third sections were composed by SUS questions to evaluate either the VR or AR interface.

To illustrate the procedure of the test, we refer to the two users participating one test session as user A and B. Each user was randomly assigned an interface (e.g., the AR one for user A and the VR one for user B). Then, both testers started playing a training session to properly understand the interfaces and the interaction paradigm. When the users feel ready, they could start a proper chess playing session, lasting 10 min. At the end of the session, each user had to complete the SUS questions related to the adopted interface (either the AR or VR one). Then, the users had to swap interfaces, play another training session to understand the interfaces functionalities and finally start another chess playing session of 10 min. Finally, each user had to complete the SUS questions related to the adopted interface (either the AR or VR one).

Tests have been evaluated with a number of participants (20) too small to obtain results with statistical validity. Despite this, the proposed study can be suitable to lay the foundations for future developments. The average score of each question and the final SUS score has been calculated using the procedure illustrated in [23]. Overall both interfaces have been evaluated to more than good on the SUS score scale (Fig. 2), so it is reasonable to consider the interfaces deployment through the proposed framework successful. However, since the AR interface has obtained a lower score, it would be useful to understand how to improve it in order to obtain a score comparable with the VR interface.

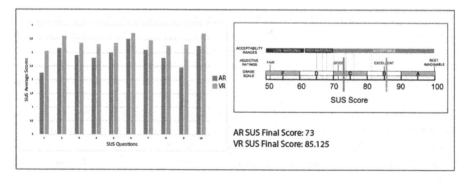

Fig. 2. The SUS average score of each question (on the left) for the AR (orange) and VR (green) interfaces. The SUS final score (on the right). (Color figure online)

One can identify several problem classes: Hardware related problem, Interaction problem and Visualization problem. The first issue is related to the AR device: since the HoloLens glasses have a very limited field-of-view (FOV) that is around 35°, testers could not watch the entire chess board at a time and they were forced to change their point of view. Moreover, the FOV limitation did not allow users to clearly detect the moves of the VR opponent. Thus, the AR player sometimes could not see that a move had been made, so he couldn't follow the game flow anymore.

The underlying reasons of the second problem can be related in a weak link between the virtual environment and the real world. In fact, the AR input modality forced the user to interact at first with the virtual world and then with the real one. It is conceivable to presume that this "double" interaction has required a substantial cognitive workload that has obliged the user to focus only on the interaction and not on the game itself. Moreover, some users had trouble executing the tap gesture to select the game pieces.

The last issue is related to the difficulty of perceiving the depth on the game field. When a virtual game piece was covered by a real one (or vice versa), the AR user was not able to realize which piece was in front of the other, forcing user to change his/her position to inspect the game board from a side view. The purpose of the virtual grid was to reduce this issue, but it was used only by two players, thus it is not possible to ascertain its effectiveness.

6 Conclusions

In this study, a novel, multiplayer game system for both AR and VR interfaces that allows players to experience the same (or similar) experience has been proposed. In order to assess the effectiveness of the system, a usability comparison between an AR interface and a VR one has been proposed. Prior works have come up with AR and VR based interfaces that are part of the same game. However, interfaces and functionalities are developed based on the specific characteristics of the input/output hardware, thus the provided game experiences are substantially different between AR and VR.

The same game experience can be conveyed to different users that are playing using different interfaces. Both interfaces have been deemed suitable for interacting with the same contents. Notwithstanding the interfaces belonged to different environments, the same functionalities were given. If for a given environment it is possible to obtain a specific interaction thanks to the software, in the other one the same interaction can be obtained thanks to the hardware. Moreover, this study suggests that it is possible to establish an effective communication between an AR and VR worlds if the experience content is independent of the hardware. Finally, the test results prove that both the overall system and the proposed AR and VR interfaces are suitable for a shared game experience. Future developments will be focused on integrating the automatic SquareOff[10] chessboard to avoid the "double" interaction of the AR player.

---

[10] https://squareoffnow.com/.

References

1. Milgram, P., Kishino, F.: A taxonomy of mixed reality visual displays. IEICE Trans. Inf. Syst. **77**(12), 1321–1329 (1994)
2. Vogel, H.L.: Entertainment Industry Economics: A Guide for Financial Analysis. Cambridge University Press, Cambridge (2014)
3. Bates, J.: Virtual reality, art, and entertainment. Presence: Teleoperators & Virtual Environments **1**(1), 133–138 (1992)
4. Stapleton, C., Hughes, C., Moshell, M., Micikevicius, P., Altman, M.: Applying mixed reality to entertainment. Computer **35**(12), 122–124 (2002)
5. Azuma, R.T: A survey of augmented reality. Presence: Teleoperators & Virtual Environments **6**(4), 355–385 (1997)
6. Newby, G.B.: Virtual reality and the entertainment industry. Bull. Am. Soc. Inf. Sci. **21**(1), 20–21 (1994)
7. Loeffler, C.E.: Distributed virtual reality: applications for education, entertainment and industry. Telektronikk **89**, 83 (1993)
8. Woodfield, R.: Virtual reality, videogames and the story of art (1996)
9. Giles, W., Schroeder, R., Cleal, B.: Virtual reality and the future of interactive games. In: Warnecke, H.J., Bullinger, H.J. (eds.) Virtual Reality 1994, pp. 377–391. Springer, Heidelberg (1994). https://doi.org/10.1007/978-3-662-10795-9_24
10. Gálvez, A., Iglesias, A.: Videogames and virtual reality as effective edutainment tools. In: Kim, T.-h., Lee, Y.-h., Kang, B.-H., Ślęzak, D. (eds.) FGIT 2010. LNCS, vol. 6485, pp. 564–576. Springer, Heidelberg (2010). https://doi.org/10.1007/978-3-642-17569-5_55
11. Burkle, M., Magee, M.: Virtual learning: videogames and virtual reality in education. In: Digital Tools for Seamless Learning, pp. 325–344. IGI Global (2017)
12. Schmalstieg, D.: Augmented reality techniques in games. In: Proceedings of the 4th IEEE/ACM International Symposium on Mixed and Augmented Reality, pp. 176–177. IEEE Computer Society (2005)
13. Szalavári, Z., Eckstein, E., Gervautz, M.: Collaborative gaming in augmented reality. In: Proceedings of the ACM symposium on Virtual Reality Software and Technology, pp. 195–204. ACM (1998)
14. Piekarski, W., Thomas, B.: ARQuake: the outdoor augmented reality gaming system. Commun. ACM **45**(1), 36–38 (2002)
15. Cheok, A.D., et al.: Human Pacman: a mobile, wide-area entertainment system based on physical, social, and ubiquitous computing. Pers. Ubiquitous Comput. **8**(2), 71–81 (2004)
16. Lindt, I., Ohlenburg, J., Pankoke-Babatz, U., Prinz, W., Ghellal, S.: Combining multiple gaming interfaces in epidemic menace. In CHI 2006 Extended Abstracts on Human Factors in Computing Systems, pp. 213–218. ACM (2006)
17. Ranade, S., Zhang, M., Al-Sada, M., Urbani, J., Nakajima, T.: Clash tanks: an investigation of virtual and augmented reality gaming experience. In: 2017 Tenth International Conference on Mobile Computing and Ubiquitous Network (ICMU), pp. 1–6. IEEE (2017)
18. Vera, L., Gimeno, J., Casas, S., García-Pereira, I., Portalés, C.: A hybrid virtual-augmented serious game to improve driving safety awareness. In: Cheok, A.D., Inami, M., Romão, T. (eds.) ACE 2017. LNCS, vol. 10714, pp. 293–310. Springer, Cham (2018). https://doi.org/10.1007/978-3-319-76270-8_21
19. Ferdinand, P., Müller, S., Ritschel, T., Wechselberger, U.: The eduventure-a new approach of digital game based learning combining virtual and mobile augmented reality games episodes. In: Pre-conference Workshop "Game based Learning" of DeLFI 2005 and GMW 2005 Conference, Rostock, vol. 13 (2005)

20. Rayar, F., Boas, D., Patrizio, R.: ART-chess: a tangible augmented reality chess on tabletop. In: Proceedings of the 2015 International Conference on Interactive Tabletops & Surfaces, pp. 229–233. ACM (2015)
21. Bikos, M., Itoh, Y., Klinker, G., Moustakas, K.: An interactive augmented reality chess game using bare-hand pinch gestures. In: 2015 International Conference on Cyberworlds (CW), pp. 355–358. IEEE (2015)
22. Fender, A., Müller, J., Lindlbauer, D.: Creature teacher: a performance-based animation system for creating cylic movements. In: Proceedings of the 3rd ACM Symposium on Spatial User Interaction, pp. 113–122. ACM (2015)
23. Brooke, J.: SUS-a quick and dirty usability scale. Usability Eval. Ind. **189**(194), 4–7 (1996)

Microbial Integration on Player Experience of Hybrid Bio-digital Games

Raphael Kim[1]([⊠]), Siobhan Thomas[2], Roland van Dierendonck[3],
Antonios Kaniadakis[1], and Stefan Poslad[1]

[1] Queen Mary University, London, UK
r.s.kim@qmul.ac.uk
[2] London South Bank University, London, UK
[3] Studio Roland van Dierendonck, Amsterdam, The Netherlands

Abstract. Hybrid bio-digital games physically integrate non-human, living organisms into computer gaming hardware and software. Whilst such type of game can add novelty value, the positive impact of the added biological element on player experience has not yet been verified quantitatively. We conducted a study involving two groups of 20 participants, to compare player experiences of two versions of a video game called *Mould Rush*, which relies on the growth patterns of micro-organisms commonly known as 'mould'. Results from self-reporting Game Experience Questionnaire (GEQ) showed that the group who played the version of *Mould Rush* that integrated real mould, had produced significantly higher mean GEQ scores ($p < .001$) on the following dimensions: *Positive Affect; Sensory and Imaginative Immersion; Positive Experience;* and *Returning to Reality.* Furthermore, results from participant interviews indicated that the slowness of mould growth was enjoyed by those who played real-mould-integrated version of *Mould Rush*. Contrastingly, the slowness was perceived as a negative feature for those who played the game without integrated mould. We discuss the implications and limitations of all of our findings.

Keywords: Hybrid gaming · Microbial integration · Bio-digital interaction

1 Introduction

In recent years, hybrid bio-digital games (hereafter called biotic games), which integrate living organisms and biological materials into computer games [1], have been gaining popularity. Amongst over 60 works that are included in van Eck's hybrid biological digital games database [2], which reference works that stretch as far back as the 1940s, almost half of them have been created only in the last decade. Such games are often driven by the intelligence of non-human organisms (e.g. slime moulds [3, 4]), which offers novel gaming experience in contrast to digital counterparts that are driven solely via computer algorithms. Biotic games also offer not two, but a three-way interaction between humans, computers, and the integrated biological agent, to be explored. However, whilst these features open up a rich design space for interactive entertainment, our current lack of understanding on how players experience games of this nature could pose challenges in meaningful improvements of their designs. More

P. Cortez et al. (Eds.): INTETAIN 2018, LNICST 273, pp. 148–159, 2019.
https://doi.org/10.1007/978-3-030-16447-8_15

specifically, the impact of integrated biological agent in experiencing computer games has not yet been empirically verified and analyzed: Does the integration positively enhance gaming experience over non-integrated equivalent, and how? In this paper, we attempt to answer these questions by presenting and discussing the results of a comparative player study involving two versions of a biotic game called *Mould Rush*[1].

Definition: we define the term 'microbial integration' as the physical presence of living micro-organisms in the game's Biotic Processing Unit (BPU) [5]. The BPU of *Mould Rush* is a modified flatbed scanner described by Kim et al. [6], designed to house the growing microbes and allow continuous imaging of their growth [7].

2 Related Works

2.1 Microbe-Integrated Systems

In Hossain's user study involving interactive cloud experimentation system and manipulation of slime moulds [8], participants expressed a preference for 'real' experiments involving live microbes, over simulations. Hossain concluded that one of the reasons behind this preference could be due to the implicit narrative attached to real systems, and that it would in turn increase the user's sense of connection to the system. In the user study of *Trap It!* [9], a touchscreen-based tool that enables playful human-microbe interaction, it was noted that some users expressed excitement upon realizing that they were interacting with real micro-organisms (*Euglena Sp.*). The study hypothesized that such realization drove user motivation and interest in further experiencing the system. In Kim's user study of *LuduScope* [10], an interactive smartphone microscopy for games with *Euglena*, revealed that when compared to computer-generated simulations, the majority of participants stated benefits of interacting with the real biology (*"It is more convincing if you have a real cell"*). Although these studies suggest that playing with real organisms would offer better playing experience (e.g. in terms of enjoyment), no comparative study involving real and simulated versions of a biotic game has yet been carried out, in order to verify this hypothesis.

2.2 Player Expectations

In van Eck and Lamers' survey on player expectations around biotic games [11], one of their conclusions stated that players expected increased enjoyment when playing against real animals (that are mediated by computers). Further findings also hinted at possible reasons why this would be the case: The majority of the respondents had expected and preferred the added unpredictability offered by the animal opponent, as well as the novelty factor that the game offered. Yet, as acknowledged by van Eck and Lamers (*"expectations are not experiences"*), a comparative empirical study on actual player experiences is called for, to verify such player expectations.

---

[1] https://biohackanddesign.com/mould_rush/.

2.3 Human vs. Algorithmic Control

In Weibel's study [12], it was found that players had experienced better presence, flow, and enjoyment whilst playing a game with human-controlled opponent, in comparison to playing with a computer-controlled one. Although the results cannot be directly used to hypothesize that similar results can be replicated with animal/microbe-controlled opponents, this is a relevant study nevertheless, as it measures well-known dimensions of player experience, comparing the effects of biological intelligence (human) and algorithmically-controlled (computer) opponents.

3 Player Experience Study

3.1 Objectives and Hypothesis

The main objective of the study was to find out how the integration of real microbes affected players' experience of a biotic game. In order to achieve this, two versions of *Mould Rush* game were tested. First version was used as a control, which did not integrate real mould in the BPU, but had only allowed players to interact with pre-recorded images of its growth. The second version allowed players to interact with real living mould as part of the game. We hypothesized that the players who play with integrated mould would have a more positive overall playing experience than those who did not.

3.2 Mould Rush Game

Overview. *Mould Rush* is a proof-of-concept, online multiplayer game used for the study. The game invites players to watch a live broadcast on *Twitch*[2], streaming a plate of micro-organisms ('mould') growing in real-time. Graphic overlays are used to divide the plate into numbered segments, which players can select during the game. The goal of the game is to collect as many microbes as possible within an allocated timeframe. Players do this by choosing a segment by typing its number on the game's chat/message box (Fig. 1). Players can also reduce the opponents' chances of collecting cells, by either preventing them from collecting cells from a segment (using *block* command), or by destroying the cells that the opponents had previously collected (using *kill* command).

Basic Rules and Scoring. The game lasts for three days. The players are permitted to submit one set of commands (*collect | block | kill*) at least once daily, and at most three times daily. Scores from each segment is calculated based on the coverage of microbes found in the segment, calculated using an image recognition script in *Open CV*. At the end of the third day, total number of microbes collected by each player is calculated, with the winner as the player with most accumulation of microbes. Comprehensive background and details of the technical set-up can be found in *Mould Rush* website1.

Versions. *Version 1:* This consists of pre-recorded timelapse of microbial growth, broken into a series of images that are shown to the player during the game. Players observe the growth and simply submit commands to collect, block, and kill cells. All commands are translated into graphical symbols, which are overlaid on top of the growth images (Fig. 2, left). Note that the growth images are updated every hour, with changes in microbial growth appearing at the same rate as the real growth. The use of pre-recorded images means that exact visual representation of mould can be achieved, and thus they are aesthetically more realistic than graphic illustrations or computer renderings. *Version 2:* This integrates real microbes into the game's BPU for game play. As such, it live broadcasts real cells growing and dying (*"live and alive mode"*) (Figs. 1 and 2, right).

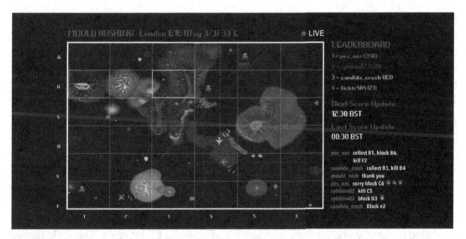

Fig. 1. Scene from a typical *Mould Rush* game version 2. Note image of microbes growing in real-time, that are divided into identifiable segments. Graphic overlays depict different commands, which are submitted by players through the game chat box (bottom right hand corner).

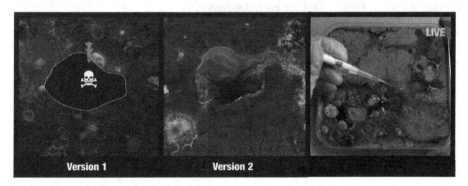

Fig. 2. Kill command in action: Version 1 (left) simulates cell killing with simple graphic overlay, whereas version 2 shows the extent of real physical destruction of cells (right) that had been carried out as part of the live broadcast by the moderator (far right).

The 'Kill' Command. When players decide to kill a segment, microbes found inside the segment are destroyed in one of two ways, depending on the version of the game played. In game version 1, the cells are destroyed virtually, only through graphic depiction (Fig. 2, left). In version 2, the cells are killed in real life, mid-livestream, by the moderator who drops an antibacterial agent (i.e. bleach) onto the segment of the growth plate (Fig. 2, far right). As a result, those playing with version 2 of the game are able to see the destroyed area in real life (Fig. 2, right).

4 Materials and Methods

4.1 Study Design

Participants. In total, 40 participants took part in the study (16 female, 26 male, mean age = 25.8, SD = 4.15). They were recruited through adverts placed in the lead author's university email list and on flyers placed around the campus. Participants were a mixture of the University students and staff. All participants received a cash incentive for participating. The participants were divided equally into two cohorts of 20. Cohort 1 played *Mould Rush* version 1 and cohort 2 played version 2 of the game.

Game Experience Questionnaire (GEQ). Developed by Ijsselsteijn et al. [13], GEQ is a self-reporting questionnaire used to measure various game-related, subjective dimensions of playing experience, which include the following. Core module: *Competence; Sensory and Imaginative Immersion; Flow; Tension/Annoyance; Challenge; Negative Affect; Positive Affect.* Post-game module: *Positive Experience; Negative Experience; Tiredness; Returning to Reality.* In order to quantify these dimensions, a set of statements that describe various feelings associated with player experience were presented to the players, for them to relate on a five-point Likert scale. The scale ranged from 0 (*Do not agree*) to 4 (*Completely agree*), with example statements including: "*I was interested in the game's story*"; "*I felt frustrated*"; and "*It was aesthetically pleasing*". The Likert ratings of each statement (50 in total) were combined in specific combinations as outlined by Ijsselsteijn et al. [13], and were subsequently averaged to provide the mean GEQ scores for each dimension.

Participant Interview. Each participant was interviewed individually after the game to discuss their experiences. In order to produce a well-rounded picture of their experience, the interviews were intended to complement the GEQ. Each interview lasted around 10 min, and were conducted either in person, via phone, *Facebook*, or *Skype*. Two open-ended questions were asked to start the interview (*Q1: How did you find the game? Q2: Tell me what you liked and disliked about this game, and why?*). Participants were asked to elaborate further if they gave single-word or ambiguous statements.

4.2 Running the Study

Briefing. Participants were given an information sheet explaining the background of the study, and a consent form to sign. They were also provided with the game rule book. Careful measures were taken to ensure that each participant was aware of their game set up, i.e., whether it allowed interaction with live micro-organisms (version 2), or not (version 1). Participants were free to log into the game at any point during the study, using a device of their choice (e.g. desktop/laptop). A day prior to the start of the game, each participant was issued with a *Twitch* account username and password which enabled them to submit commands on the chat box.

Game Set-Up and Scheduling. A pilot study with four unpaid volunteers from the University was carried out prior to the main study, to ensure consistent game operation. Each game consisted of four competing participants and a moderator (i.e., the lead author). The first day was practice day, to help participants to familiarize with the game and ask any questions to the moderator. The second and third days were proper game days. Each day started at 12:30 BST and ended at 00:30 BST. Score updates were made at the following times: 12:30 BST, 18:30 BST, and 00:30 BST. The moderator was responsible for (a) streaming the game on *Twitch*, (b) moderating chat box messages, (c) culturing live micro-organisms for version 2 of the game, and (d) destroying micro-organisms to process the *kill* commands. The microbes were cultured in a laboratory environment, and participants were not physically exposed to the cells during the study.

5 Results

5.1 Mean GEQ Scores

All participants ($N = 40$) had completed the GEQ after each game. Mean GEQ scores of 11 player experience dimensions were calculated using the GEQ scoring system [13] and are presented in Fig. 3. An independent t-test was conducted to compare the mean GEQ scores produced between the two cohorts. Significance threshold was set at .05. All positive dimensions were shown to be significantly higher in mean GEQ scores in cohort 2 than in cohort 1 (Fig. 3). This result suggests that when players interact with live organisms during the game of Mould Rush, their experiences are positively enhanced. The complete set of t-values and p-values for all dimension are outlined below, with the dimensions ordered in decreasing significance between the two cohorts.

Confirming our hypothesis, the mean GEQ scores show that the players who played Mould Rush with microbial integration had an overall more positive playing experience than those who did not.

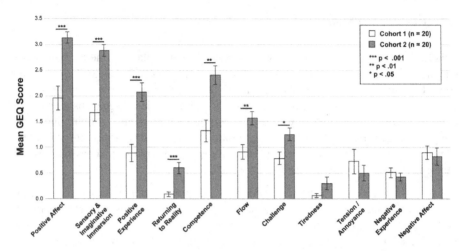

Fig. 3. Mean GEQ scores of 11 player experience dimensions between cohort 1 and 2. Standard error bars are shown. The dimensions are ordered in the order of decreasing significance in terms of their differences in mean GEQ scores between cohorts 1 and 2. **Positive Affect:** Cohort 1 (M = 1.96, SD = 1.03), Cohort 2 (M = 3.13, SD = 0.48); t(38) = 4.49, $p < .001$. **Sensory and Imaginative Immersion**: Cohort 1 (M = 1.67, SD = 0.76), Cohort 2 (M = 2.88, SD = 0.51); t(38) = 5.66, $p < .001$. **Positive Experience:** Cohort 1 (M = 0.89, SD = 0.75), Cohort 2 (M = 2.07, SD = 0.80); t(38) = 4.42, $p < .001$. **Returning to Reality:** Cohort 1 (M = 0.09, SD = 0.20), Cohort 2 (M = 0.60, SD = 0.48); t(38) = 3.88, $p < .001$. **Competence:** Cohort 1 (M = 1.32, SD = 0.97), Cohort 2 (M = 2.40, SD = 0.81); t(38) = 3.59, $p = .001$. **Flow:** Cohort 1 (M = 0.92, SD = 0.63), Cohort 2 (M = 1.57, SD = 0.57); t(38) = 3.19, $p = .003$. **Challenge:** Cohort 1 (M = 0.79, SD = 0.54), Cohort 2 (M = 1.25, SD = 0.54); t(38) = 2.50, $p = .018$. **Tiredness:** Cohort 1 (M = 0.07, SD = 0.18), Cohort 2 (M = 0.30, SD = 0.55); t(38) = 1.58, $p = .12$. **Tension/Annoyance:** Cohort 1 (M = 0.73, SD = 1.07), Cohort 2 (M = 0.50, SD = 0.69); t(38) = −0.78, $p = .44$. **Negative Experience:** Cohort 1 (M = 0.51, SD = 0.46), Cohort 2 (M = 0.43, SD = 0.34); t(38) = −0.57, $p = .57$. **Negative Affect:** Cohort 1 (M = 0.90, SD = 0.56), Cohort 2 (M = 0.83, SD = 0.74); t(38) = −0.33, $p = .75$.

5.2   Participant Interviews

15 out of 20 participants from cohort 1 took part in the post-game interview (M = 9.17 min) which was conducted over *Skype* (60%) and telephone (40%). All participants from cohort 2 took part in the post-game interview (M = 10.37 min) which was conducted over *Skype* (30%), telephone (20%) and *Facebook* messenger (50%). Participant responses were categorized into themes, and ranked according to their popularity[3]. An emoticon was assigned for each theme according to the nature of the majority of the opinions expressed (☺ = mostly positive ☹ = mostly negative ☺ = equally positive and negative). An abbreviated summary of the results is shown in Tables 1 and 2.

---

[3] Only the top 8 most popular themes have been presented in this paper for brevity.

Table 1. Abbreviated summary of cohort 1 interviews

Rank	Theme	☺ / ☹	Typical Remark
1	Game Rules	☹	*"I didn't like long periods between score updates"*
2	Slowness	☹	*"Lack of immediate response from cells was frustrating"*
3	Visuals	☺	*"The cells looked real and impressive"*
4	Other	☺	*"I felt disappointed, no sense of achievement or euphoria"*
5	Tangibility	☹	*"I felt very distant from the game"*
6	Unpredictability	☺	*"I liked random shapes that the cells were producing"*
7	Novelty	-	None
8	Narrative	-	None

Table 2. Abbreviated summary of cohort 2 interviews

Rank	Theme	☺ / ☹	Typical Remark
1	Other	☺	*"It was fascinating"*
2	Slowness	☺	*"I enjoyed seeing the mould culture develop over time"*
3	Game Rules	☹	*"Space is too limited for full gaming experience"*
4	Visuals	☺	*"The mould produced great colours and shapes"*
5	Novelty	☺	*"A game with an unknown rule set! (microbial growth)"*
6	Unpredictability	☺	*"Relying on randomness of microbes was satisfying"*
7	Tangibility	☺	*"I liked the fact that it was against a real organism"*
8	Narrative	☺	*"Watching cells being killed added layer to the story"*

Common and Contrasting Themes Between the Two Cohorts. As deducted from Tables 1 and 2, there were five mutual themes. Among them, *Game Rules*, *Visuals*, and *Unpredictability* had shared the same perception (negative), whereas *Slowness* and *Tangibility* were expressed in contrasting manners between the two cohorts.

6 Discussion

6.1 Mean GEQ Scores and Interview Data

Whilst it is impractical to elaborate on all 11 dimensions that has been measured by GEQ, below we highlight the ones with most compelling implications, for discussion. These are also cross-referenced with the interview data to corroborate our arguments.

Sensory and Imaginative Immersion. As one of the most significantly enhanced GEQ dimension measured in cohort 2 in comparison with cohort 1, one component statement that forms this dimension include *"I was interested in the game's story"*.

This finding supports Hossain's assessment that real systems have implicit narrative attached to them, making it attractive for players to connect with them [8]. In addition to a typical interview remark mentioned in Table 2, the strong sense of narrative felt by the players are also reflected in comments such as *"Showing us the growth plate, and the ritual of killing cells as part of the gameplay, add to the story and makes the game special"*.

Negative Experiences. Interestingly, none of the negative dimensions from the GEQ (*Tiredness; Tension/Annoyance; Negative Experience; Negative Affect*) showed significant differences between the two cohorts (Fig. 3). The interview data points at three common problematic features of *Mould Rush* game encountered by both cohorts that may explain the phenomena. First one concerns the lack of immediacy in interactivity (*"Sometimes the progress could not be seen in real-time and that was frustrating. As gamers, we are used to seeing actions in real-time."*). The second feature was the lack of clarity in rules (*"I wasn't quite sure how you defined a microbe within a cell to calculate the scores. Because they look so ambiguous, I'm not sure if the scoring system is entirely fair"*). And thirdly, the lack of time given for strategizing (*"The timescale was too short to formulate a strategy and to gauge other players' styles"*).

Based on this, we may speculate that the very integration of real microbes in *Mould Rush* version 2 have not been directly responsible for participants' negative experience.

Further inferences may be made that the addition of real biological element can at best add value to the game, but at worst do not contribute towards negative experience.

However, caution must be exercised when interpreting this observation, as none of the participants had experience of playing biotic games before, and that novelty-bias may have masked out negative aspects of *Mould Rush* game.

Contrasting Perception of Slowness. The interviews revealed a striking contrast between the two cohorts in how they perceived the slow real-time microbial growth. Whilst the two versions of the game ran at the same speed (i.e. rates of growth were both depicted in real-time), those who played with real microbes felt that the slowness was a contributing factor towards enjoyment (*"I looked forward to taking a peep occasionally throughout the day and see small landscape changes happen"*), whereas those who did not, had felt that slowness was a hindrance (*"I felt frustrated by the lack of dynamic changes on the screen"*). Further still, one participant from cohort 1 remarked, *"If I could play with real microbes, I would have enjoyed it more as I would have treated it like gardening, or even real hunting (of animals to catch)"*. We hypothesize that the realization by the players that they are playing with real organisms alters their perception of slowness, perhaps by increasing their tolerance to slow game dynamics, or by associating it to another leisure activity where slowness is expected.

Microbial Aesthetics (Visuals). One of the most consistent and popular remarks made by participants from both cohorts was the visual aspect of *Mould Rush* (*"Growth patterns of mould were colourful and stunning"; "The weird and wonderful shapes they (mould) produced, I felt that I was on an alien planet"*). This is a promising observation which offers an empirical evidence to support Gerber's recommendation [5] in designing effective hybrid bio-digital games (*"The biological features of interest should be highlighted to the player"*).

6.2   Bio-ethics

During the interview with cohort 2, who had played *Mould Rush* with real microbes, only one participant (5%) had raised concerns about the ethical aspects of the game (*"Maybe it would have been better to label 'kill' commands as 'attack' or 'destroy' commands, as I felt uncomfortable being reminded that I was killing living things as part of a game"*). Such low number was surprising given that the game involved manipulation (i.e. killing) of living cells for the sake of entertainment. This notion had previously attracted several types of ethical criticisms from the general public, who were reacting to Riedel-Kruse's game involving *Paramecia* [14]. We hypothesize that the lack of ethical concern displayed with our study may be influenced by the type of microbial species that were being gamified. Whilst Riedel-Kruse's *Paramecia* are motile and thus display a more animal-like quality, the idea of manipulating mould may less distressing, especially given the negative perception (and apathy) they receive in mainstream media, for instance in adverts for cleaning products. Furthermore, we hypothesize that the remoteness of the microbes' location in relation to the players during gameplay, which had prevented them from physically interacting with microbes, may have reduced potential ethical concerns being raised within the players' minds.

6.3   Limitations of the Study

Whilst the implementation of the GEQ had produced a general overview of player experience, the findings may not entirely reflect the experiences that may have been derived exclusively from human-microbe interactions. Since the GEQ had been mainly designed to evaluate conventional computer games (with humans and computers only) [13], experiences associated with non-human biological presence and potential bio-ethical dilemma were not explicitly measured. Therefore, we acknowledge that additional set of questions, included either as an extension to the GEQ and/or the post-game interview, would be beneficial in obtaining a more accurate picture for similar studies in the future. Furthermore, given the high diversity of organisms and interfaces deployed across biotic games [2], we recognize that the findings from our single game-based study may not offer insights that can be translated to all biotic games. As such, we propose that designers approach evaluation of biotic games on a game-by-game, and a species-by-species basis.

6.4   Wider Implications

Micro-organisms are common workhorses of synthetic biology [15], and they are likely to increase in significance as the technology advances with time. For example, the increasing sophistication and accessibility of gene editing techniques such as *CRISPR/Cas9* [16] means that in the future, biotic game designers could build and customize their game characters genetically with an unprecedented granularity. As such, we anticipate a notable increase in the use of microbes in biotic game designs in the next few years, and that this paper can serve as a relevant and insightful case study.

6.5 Further Work

We aim to use our findings as a starting point to further our investigations on specific areas of bio-digital gaming experience. For instance, the contrasting reactions of players from the two different cohorts on slowness of interactivity, will motivate us in testing our hypothesis that the slowness of microbial growth is tolerated (and perhaps even enjoyed) when real organisms are integrated into computer games.

Additionally, *Mould Rush* is an uncommon type of biotic game, in the sense that it resides within the Internet of Things (IoT) framework, which focusses on the connectedness of an increasing range of physical things via smart devices [17]. Through connecting micro-organisms to an online gaming platform *Twitch*, *Mould Rush* provides an opportunity to investigate the effects of remote gameplay and indirect biological manipulation on player experience, as well as on a wider range of socio-cultural benefits that IoT applications can potentially bring [18, 19].

7 Conclusion

Overall, our study was the first of its kind in scientifically and empirically comparing the feelings and perceptions of players who had engaged in biologically-integrated and non-integrated forms of computer gaming. The findings confirm our initial hypothesis that playing with live interactive function with integration of real micro-organisms enhance the playing experiences of the gamer, in contrast to playing the game's equivalent without integrated micro-organisms. Furthermore, we report on the possible reasons behind such enhancement of player experience. This includes (but not exclusive to): Enhanced narrative through sensory and imaginative immersion, and aesthetic enjoyment through unique visual growth patterns produced by microbial growth. We propose that such observations can be a helpful indicator towards better design of games of this nature, as designers can increase their focus on enhancing their game's narrative, and by highlighting special biological features that are impractical to be emulated or simulated by computers. We also report on significant interview results that can form the basis for further investigation. More specifically, the concept of slowness and how they are perceived between real and simulated gaming is a potentially promising avenue for further investigation. This paper also highlights the need to formulate biology-specific models, to measure player experiences more accurately, which ultimately would help better understanding of bio-digital games in the future and progress the field forward.

Acknowledgements. This research was supported by EPSRC and AHRC Centre for Doctoral Training in Media and Arts Technology (EP/L01632X/1).

References

1. Riedel-Kruse, I.H., Chung, A.M., Dura, B., Hamilton, A.L., Lee, B.C.: Design, engineering and utility of biotic games. Lab Chip **11**(1), 14–22 (2011). https://doi.org/10.1039/C0LC00399A
2. Database: Hybrid Biological Digital Games. https://biodigitalgames.com/database/
3. Jabr, F.: How brainless slime molds redefine intelligence. Nat. News. (2012). https://doi.org/10.1038/nature.2012.11811
4. Slime Mold Andi. https://medium.com/@slime_mold_Andi
5. Gerber, L.C., Kim, H., Riedel-Kruse, I.H.: Interactive biotechnology: design rules for integrating biological matter into digital games. In: DiGRA/FDG (2016)
6. Kim, R., Thomas, S., van Dierendonck, R., Poslad, S.: A new mould rush: designing for a slow bio-digital game driven by living micro-organisms. In: Proceedings of the 13th International Conference on the Foundations of Digital Games (FDG 2018) (2018). https://doi.org/10.1145/3235765.3235798
7. van Eck, W., Lamers, M.H.: Biological content generation: evolving game terrains through living organisms. In: Johnson, C., Carballal, A., Correia, J. (eds.) EvoMUSART 2015. LNCS, vol. 9027, pp. 224–235. Springer, Cham (2015). https://doi.org/10.1007/978-3-319-16498-4_20
8. Hossain, Z., et al.: Interactive cloud experimentation for biology: an online education case study. In: Proceedings of the 33rd Annual ACM Conference on Human Factors in Computing Systems (2015). https://doi.org/10.1145/2702123.2702354
9. Lee, S.A., et al.: Trap it!: a playful human-biology interaction for a museum installation. In: Proceedings of 33rd Annual ACM Conference on Human Factors in Computing Systems (2015). https://doi.org/10.1145/2702123.2702220
10. Kim, H., et al.: LudusScope: accessible interactive smartphone microscopy for life-science education. PLoS One **11**(10), e0162602 (2016). https://doi.org/10.1371/journal.pone.0162602
11. van Eck, W., Lamers, M.H.: Player expectations of animal incorporated computer games. In: Chisik, Y., Holopainen, J., Khaled, R., Luis Silva, J., Alexandra Silva, P. (eds.) INTETAIN 2017. LNICST, vol. 215, pp. 1–15. Springer, Cham (2018). https://doi.org/10.1007/978-3-319-73062-2_1
12. Weibel, D., Wissmath, B., Habegger, S., Steiner, Y., Groner, R.: Playing online games against computer-vs. human-controlled opponents: effects on presence, flow, and enjoyment. Comput. Hum. Behav. **24**(5), 2274–2291 (2008). https://doi.org/10.1016/j.chb.2007.11.002
13. IJsselsteijn, W.A., de Kort, Y.A.W., Poels, K.: The Game Experience Questionnaire. Technische Universiteit, Eindhoven (2013)
14. Harvey, H., Havard, M., Magnus, D., Cho, M.K., Riedel-Kruse, I.H.: Innocent fun or 'microslavery'? Hastings Cent. Rep. **44**(6), 38–46 (2014). https://doi.org/10.1002/hast.386
15. Zhang, W., Nielson, D.R.: Synthetic biology applications in industrial microbiology. Front. Microbiol. **5** (2014). https://doi.org/10.3389/fmicb.2014.00451
16. Adli, M.: The CRISPR tool kit for genome editing and beyond. Nat. Commun. **9**, 1911 (2018)
17. Poslad, S.: Ubiquitous Computing: Smart Devices, Environments and Interactions. Wiley, Hoboken (2009)
18. Charlton, P., Poslad, S.: A sharable wearable maker community IoT application. In: 12th International Conference on Intelligent Environments, IE 2016 (2016)
19. Poslad, S., Ma, A., Wang, Z., Mei, H.: Using a smart city IoT to incentivise and target shifts in mobility behaviour – is it a piece of pie? Sensors **15**(6), 13069–13096 (2015)

Author Index

Printed in the United States
By Bookmasters